The Paragraph

EFFECTIVE Academic Writing

SECOND EDITION

Alice Savage
Masoud Shafiei

OXFORD
UNIVERSITY PRESS

198 Madison Avenue
New York, NY 10016 USA

Great Clarendon Street, Oxford, ox2 6dp, United Kingdom

Oxford University Press is a department of the University of Oxford. It furthers the University's objective of excellence in research, scholarship, and education by publishing worldwide. Oxford is a registered trade mark of Oxford University Press in the UK and in certain other countries

First published in 2012

2016 2015 2014 2013

10 9 8 7 6 5 4 3

General Manager, American ELT: Laura Pearson
Publisher: Stephanie Karras
Associate Publishing Manager: Sharon Sargent
Managing Editor: Jennifer Meldrum
Director, ADP: Susan Sanguily
Executive Design Manager: Maj-Britt Hagsted
Associate Design Manager: Michael Steinhofer
Image Manager: Trisha Masterson
Electronic Production Manager: Julie Armstrong
Production Artist: Elissa Santos
Production Coordinator: Chris Espejo
Production Coordinator: Brad Tucker

ISBN: 978 0 19 432346 8 Effective Academic Writing 1 with Online Practice pack

ISBN: 978 0 19 432341 3 Effective Academic Writing 1 Student Book as pack component

ISBN: 978 0 19 433391 7 Effective Academic Writing Online

Printed in China

This book is printed on paper from certified and well-managed sources

ACKNOWLEDGEMENTS

The authors and publisher are grateful to those who have given permission to reproduce the following extracts and adaptations of copyright material:

p. 31 Excerpts from "Sari of the Gods" from *Sari of the Gods* by G. S. Sharat Chandra, 1998, Coffee House Press. Used by permission; p. 55 From *Galileo Galilei: First Physicist* by James MacLachlan. Copyright © 1999 Oxford University Press. By permission of Oxford University Press, Inc.; p. 105 From *A House for Mr. Biswas* by V.S. Naipaul, 1961. Reprinted by permission of Wylie Agency.

We would also like to thank the following for permission to reproduce the following photographs:

Cover, Viennaslide/Alamy; viii, Marcin Krygier/iStockphoto (laptop); p. vi, Opener, Writing Process and Review pages, 149 stocksnapper/istockphoto (letter texture); p.1 John Henley/Blend Images/Getty Images; p. 2 John Henley/Blend Images/Getty Images (coffee), p. 2 Alex Mares-Manton/Getty Images (laptop), p. 2 Tetra Images/Oxford University Press (library), p. 2 OJO Images Ltd/Alamy (classroom); p. 29 David Turnley/Corbis UK Ltd.; p. 30 David Turnley/Corbis UK Ltd.; pp. 50, 74, 100, 128, 151 Monkey Business Images/Shutterstock (Clock); p. 53 JOHN SANFORD/Science Photo Library/Getty Images; p. 54 amana images inc./Alamy (drawing), p. 54 JOHN SANFORD/Science Photo Library/Getty Images (constellation); p. 77 Willyam Bradberry/Shutterstock; p. 78 Willyam Bradberry/Shutterstock; p. 103 Daniel Valla FRPS/Alamy; p. 104 Daniel Valla FRPS/Alamy (village), p. 104 MBI/Alamy (bikes), p. 104 Joshua Roper/Alamy (orchard); p. 131 Stock Connection Blue/Alamy; p. 132 Stock Connection Blue/Alamy.

Reviewers

We would like to acknowledge the following individuals for their input during the development of the series:

Chris Alexis, College of Applied Sciences, Sur, Oman

Amina Saif Mohammed Al Hashamia, College of Applied Sciences, Nizwa, Oman

Amal Al Muqarshi, College of Applied Sciences, Ibri, Oman

Saleh Khalfan Issa Al-Rahbi, College of Applied Sciences, Nizwa, Oman

Dr. Debra Baldwin, UPP, Alfaisal University, Saudi Arabia

Virginia L. Bouchard, George Mason University, English Language Institute, Washington D.C.

Judith Buckman, College of Applied Sciences, Salalah, Oman

Dr. Catherine Buon, American University of Armenia, Armenia

Mei-Rong Alice Chen, National Taiwan University of Science and Technology, Taipei

Mark L. Cummings, Jefferson Community and Technical College, KY

Hitoshi Eguchi, Hokusei Gakuen University, Japan

Elizabeth W. Foss, Washtenaw Community College, MI

Sally C. Gearhart, Santa Rosa Junior College, CA

Alyona Gorokhova, Miramar Community College, CA

Dr. Simon Green, College of Applied Sciences, Oman

Janis Hearn, Hongik University, South Korea

Adam Henricksen, University of Maryland, Baltimore County, MD

Clay Hindman, Sierra College, CA

Kuei-ping Vicky Hsu, National Tsing Hua University, Hsinchu

Azade Johnson, Abu Dhabi Men's College, Higher Colleges of Technology, U.A.E.

Chandra Johnson, Fresno Pacific University, CA

Pei-Lun Kao, Chang Gung University, Gueishan

Yuko Kobayashi, Tokyo University of Science, Japan

Blair Lee, Kyung Hee University, Japan

Chia-yu Lin, National Tsing Hua University, Hsinchu

Kent McClintock, Chosun University, South Korea

Joan Oakley, College of the North Atlantic-Qatar, Qatar

Fernanda G. Ortiz, CESL University of Arizona, AZ

William D. Phelps, Southern Illinois University, IL

Dorothy Ramsay, College of Applied Sciences, Sohar, Oman

Vidya Rangachari, Mission College, CA

Elizabeth Rasmussen, Northern Virginia Community College, VA

Syl Rice, Abu Dhabi Men's College, Higher Colleges of Technology, U.A.E.

Donna Schaeffer, University of Washington, WA

Dr. Catherine Schaff-Stump, Kirkwood Community College, IA

Mary-Jane Scott, Sungshin Women's University, South Korea

Jenay Seymour, Hong-ik University, South Korea

Janet Sloan Rachidi, U.A.E. University, Al Ain, U.A.E.

Bob Studholme, U.A.E. University, Al Ain, U.A.E.

Paula Suzuki, SI-UK Language Centre, Japan

Sabine Thépaut, Intensive English Language Institute, University of North Texas, TX

Shu-Hui Yu, Ling Tung University, Taichung

Author Acknowledgments

We would like to thank OUP's Sharon Sargeant for giving us the opportunity to write books we believe in. Thanks also to Vicky Aeschbacher who has been the best partner anyone could hope for in an editor. We enjoyed the process every step of the way. Alex Regan and Jennifer Meldrum deserve thanks also for guiding us along the way. Always, we must express gratitude for the students who work so hard, and to our kids, Cyrus and Kaveh, who let us stay on the computer a little longer than we should.

Masoud and Alice

Contents

Unit	Academic Focus	Rhetorical Focus	Language and Grammar Focus
5 **Narrative Paragraphs** page 103	**Psychology**	• Narrative organization • Sensory and emotional details	• Order of events in narrative paragraphs • The simple past • The past continuous
6 **Opinion Paragraphs** page 131	**Urban Studies**	• Opinion organization • Reasons to support an opinion	• *There is / There are* to introduce facts • *Because of* and *because* to give reasons

APPENDICES

Welcome to Effective Academic Writing

Effective Academic Writing, Second Edition **instills student confidence and provides the tools necessary for successful academic writing.**

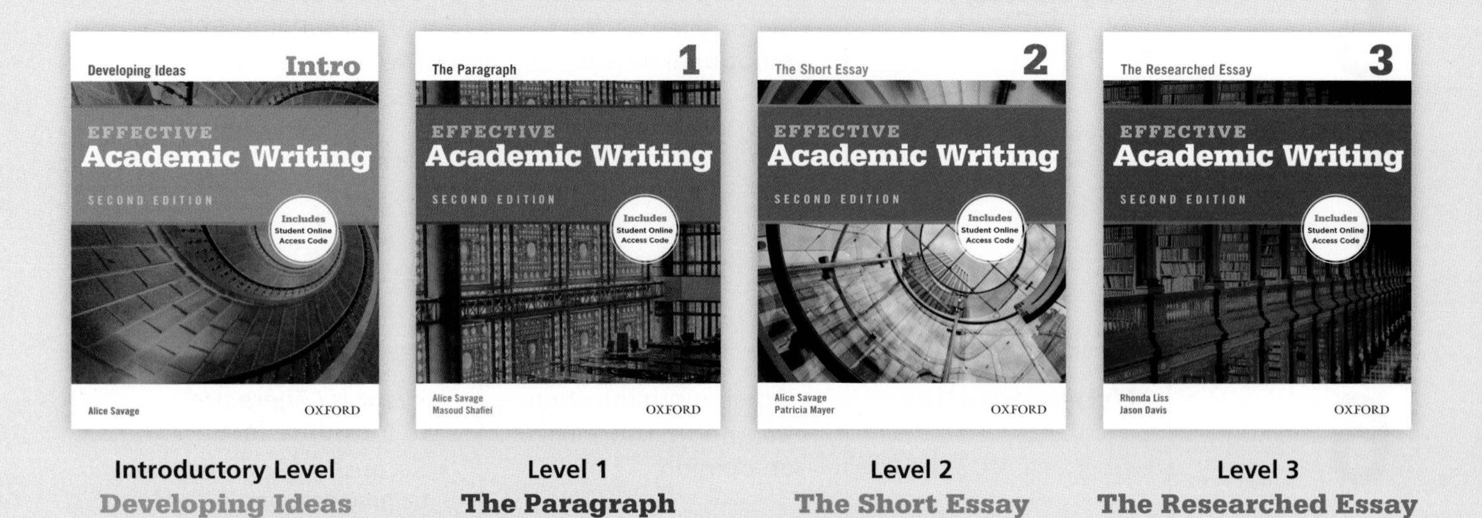

Introductory Level	Level 1	Level 2	Level 3
Developing Ideas	**The Paragraph**	**The Short Essay**	**The Researched Essay**

- Step-by-step **Writing Process** guides and refines writing skills.
- **Timed writing** practice prepares students for success on high-stakes tests.
- **Online Writing Tutor** improves academic writing inside and outside the classroom.

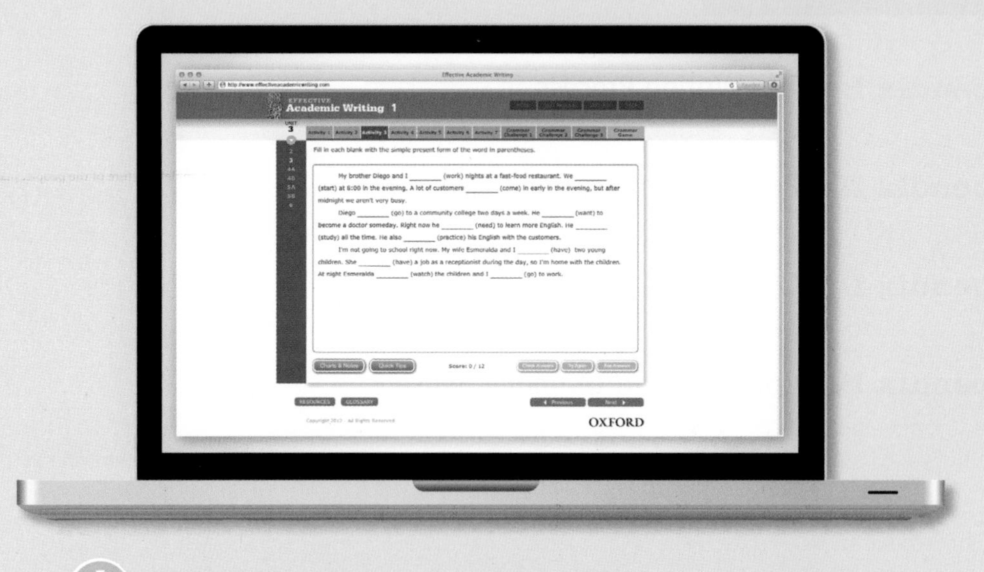

GO ONLINE

Online Writing Support for all Levels

Overview

***Effective Academic Writing, Second Edition* delivers practice that will improve your students' writing.**

- NEW! The new **Introductory Level** provides students with the support and instruction they need for writing success in the lowest-level writing courses.
- NEW! **More content-area related assignments** with more academic vocabulary and readings prepare students for the challenges of the academic classroom.

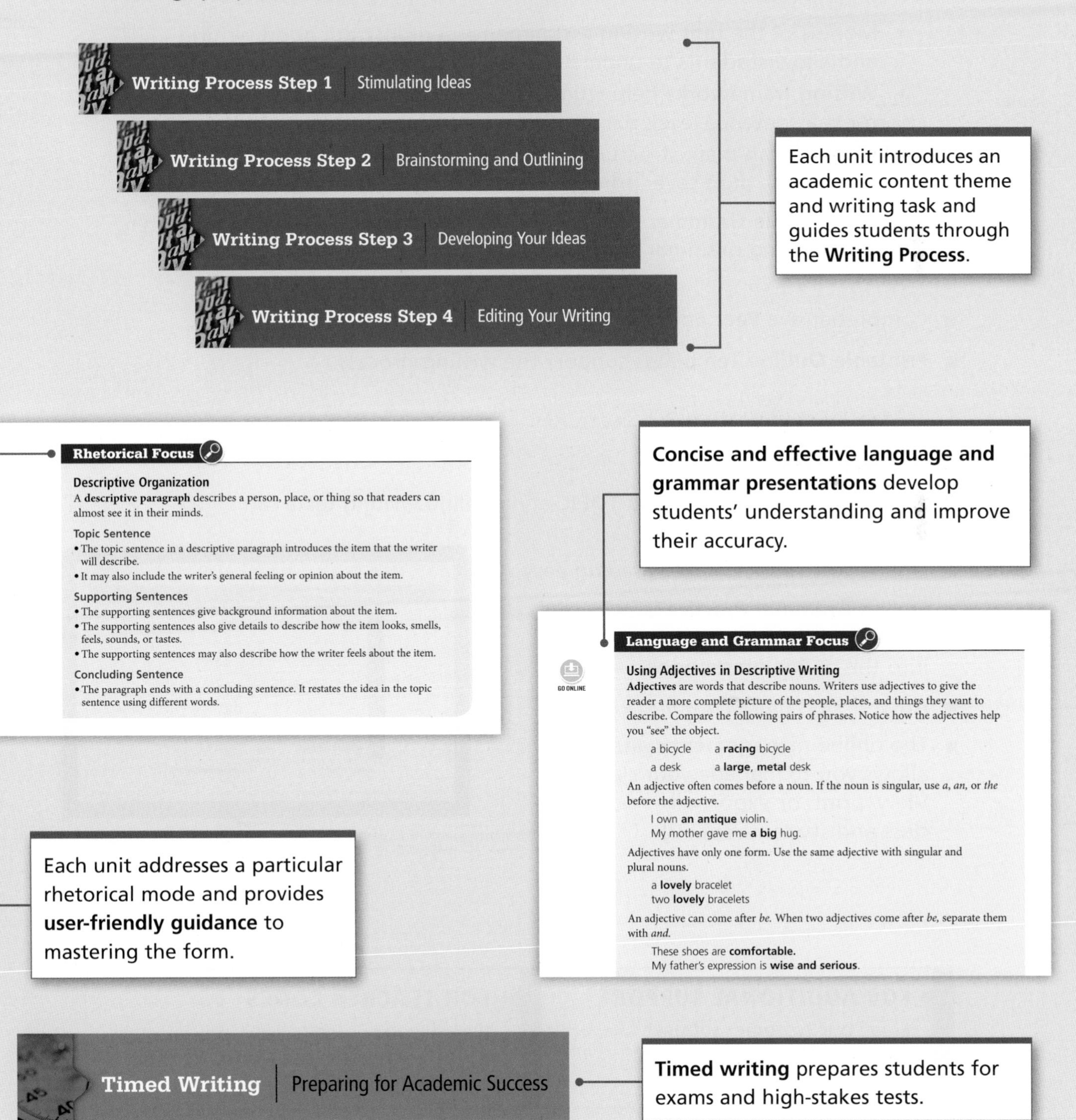

Effective Academic Writing **Online**

IT'S EASY! Use the access code printed on the inside back cover of this book to register at www.effectiveacademicwriting.com.

For the Student

- ***Online Writing Tutor*** helps students retain and apply their writing skills.
  - Models of the unit writing assignments **demonstrate good writing** and allow students to understand how each text is constructed.
  - **Writing frameworks help students with organizing and structuring,** for the sentence level, paragraph level, and the text as a whole.
  - Students can plan, structure, and write their own texts, check their work, **then save, print, or send directly to their teacher.**
- Extensive **Online Grammar Practice** and **grammar term glossary** support students in using grammar structures appropriately and fluently in their writing.
- Comprehensive **Peer Editor's Checklists** support collaborative learning.
- **Printable Outline Templates** support the writing process.

For the Teacher

- **IELTS-style, TOEFL-style, and TOEIC-style online writing tests** can be **customized** and **printed**
- **Online test rubrics** makes grading easy.
- **Online Grammar Practice** is automatically graded and entered into the online grade book.
- Answer keys makes grading easy.
- The **online management system** allows you to manage your classes. View, print, or export all class and student reports.

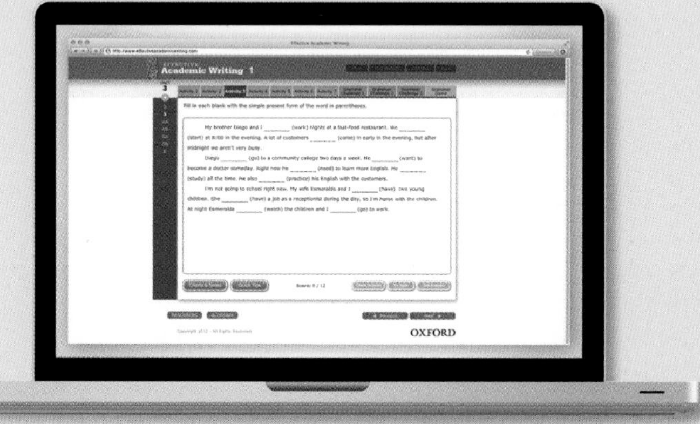

FOR ADDITIONAL SUPPORT

Email our customer support team at eltsupport@oup.com.

FOR TEACHER CODES

Please contact your sales representative for a **Teacher Access Code**. Teacher Access Codes are sold separately.

UNIT 1

The Sentence and the Paragraph

Academic Focus | Writing

Unit Goals

Rhetorical Focus

- paragraph organization
- format of a paragraph
- topic sentences, supporting sentences, and concluding sentences
- unity and coherence in a paragraph

Language and Grammar Focus

- simple sentence structure
- capitalization and end punctuation
- fragments and run-on sentences

Writing Process Part 1 | Stimulating Ideas

Exercise 1 Thinking about the topic

Discuss the pictures with a partner.

- What do the photos tell you about writing?
- What do photos A and C tell you about writing?
- What do photos B and D tell you about writing?
- How and where do you prefer to write?
- What part of writing is easier for you, finding a topic, writing drafts, or revising and editing your writing?

Rhetorical Focus

The Paragraph

A **paragraph** is a group of sentences about a topic. In this book, you will learn how to organize and write the following kinds of paragraphs.

- A **descriptive paragraph** describes a person, a place, or a thing. The writer uses clear details that will help readers imagine the subject.
- An **example paragraph** gives examples to explain a topic. The writer uses very specific examples so that the reader can clearly understand the writer's ideas.
- A **process paragraph** gives steps to tell readers how to complete a process or a task.
- A **narrative paragraph** tells a story. It is often written in the order in which events occurred.
- An **opinion paragraph** expresses beliefs or opinions about a topic. The writer tries to present reasons that will persuade readers to agree with the opinion.

Format of a Paragraph

Red

I love the color red. No other color symbolizes so many different emotions and experiences. Life would be very boring without the color red. Fires would not burn in the same way. The sunset would not be interesting, and blood would not be so surprisingly beautiful. Red is powerful when it appears in nature, and it is also powerful when it appears in our emotions. Red is love. Red is anger. Red is beauty. I like to live life in a strong way, so I think I will always admire the color red.

Exercise 2 Identifying the elements of a paragraph

A. Find the mistakes in the format of the following paragraph.

My Favorite Color

My favorite color is blue.
The color blue makes me happy.
It reminds me of the blue sky when there are no clouds and no pollution.
I think about the beaches of the Caribbean islands.
That is why my house is blue.
Blue also helps me relax. When I have a problem, I sit in my favorite chair. I look at the blue living room. I close my eyes, and I imagine the beach of a Caribbean island. My problems go away. I feel peaceful.

B. Rewrite the paragraph in the correct format.

In **Writing Process Part 2** you will . . .

- learn about paragraph organization.
- learn to write effective topic sentences.
- learn about supporting sentences.
- learn to write concluding sentences.

Rhetorical Focus

Paragraph Organization

A well-written paragraph has a **topic sentence, supporting sentences,** and a **concluding sentence.**

- The **topic sentence** introduces the topic. It also tells what the writer will say about the topic.
- The **supporting sentences** follow the topic sentence. They give more information to explain and support the topic sentence.
- The **concluding sentence** often repeats the information in the topic sentence in a different way. It may also include what the writer has learned or why the topic is important. Sometimes the concluding sentence offers a prediction, a request, or a warning.

Exercise 1 Reading a student paragraph

Read the narrative paragraph below. Notice the topic sentence, supporting sentences, and concluding sentence. What scared the barefoot boy?

Barefoot Boy

topic sentence

I had a scary experience when I was a young boy. One evening while my parents were eating dinner, I was playing barefoot in the yard with my toys. Even now I still remember the perfume of the flowers and the moisture of the grass. While I was sitting on the grass and playing with a truck, I looked up at the sky, and my attention was distracted by the beauty of the stars. Then I felt something cold and smooth slide over my feet. I stayed perfectly still, but I looked down at my feet. Then I saw a snake slowly slithering over my toes. I felt terrible and afraid, and my heart beat very fast. After the snake moved away, I screamed to my parents for help. They captured the snake and took it away. The experience frightened me, and I never went outside barefoot again.

supporting sentences

concluding sentence

Exercise 2 Examining the student paragraph

Respond to the paragraph by answering the following questions.

1. How do the supporting sentences explain the topic sentence?

____

____

2. Read the conclusion again. What did the writer learn from the experience?

____

____

Rhetorical Focus

The Topic Sentence

The **topic sentence** is usually the first or second sentence in a paragraph. It introduces a new idea. It presents the topic and explains what the writer will say about the topic. This explanation is called the **controlling idea.**

Read the following topic sentences. In each one, the topic is *my friend*. The controlling idea in each sentence explains what the writer will say about the topic. These controlling ideas tell the reader what to expect in the supporting sentences.

topic	controlling idea
My friend	is an honest person.
My friend	is the funniest person I know.
My friend	has a terribly dangerous job.

Features of an Effective Topic Sentence

A topic sentence is not a **fragment.** It is a complete sentence.

Fragment: x Smart phones for college students. (INCORRECT)
Complete Sentence: Smart phones have several useful features for college students.

A topic sentence is not too general.

Too General: Smart phones are good.
Improved: Smart phones improve communication among friends and family members.

A topic sentence is not a simple fact or specific detail.

Too Specific: Smart phones cost $300.
Improved: Because smart phones are expensive, people should consider several factors before buying one.

Exercise 3 Identifying topics and controlling ideas

In each topic sentence, circle the topic. Then underline the controlling idea.

1. (Hiking) is the best way to explore nature closely.
2. My uncle had a frightening experience as a young man.
3. Text messaging has become popular among teenagers.
4. Effective time management requires four easy steps.
5. College students drop classes for three reasons.

Exercise 4 Identifying effective topic sentences

Check (✓) the topic sentences that are effective. Revise the topic sentences that are not effective.

_____ 1. The population of my country is now 10 million.

My country's large population is a problem.

_____ 2. There are four simple steps to preparing fried rice.

_____ 3. Video games are good.

_____ 4. Exercise benefits health.

_____ 5. Eating together helps improve family relationships.

_____ 6. Homework should be optional in college.

Exercise 5 Writing topic sentences

Use each word or phrase below to write a topic sentence with a controlling idea. Then share your sentences with a partner.

1. traveling to a foreign country Traveling to a foreign country helps people learn about different cultures.
2. traffic ______________________________
3. my hometown ______________________________
4. soccer ______________________________
5. how to lose weight ______________________________

Rhetorical Focus

Supporting Sentences

Supporting sentences add information about the topic and the controlling idea.

Supporting sentences can include **definitions**, **explanations**, and **examples**.

Read the topic sentence below. Then study the types of supporting sentences that might follow.

topic | controlling idea

Young people are too dependent on computers.

Supporting Definition

Dependency on computers means that young people cannot perform normal life functions without computers.

Supporting Explanation

In the past, people memorized important information. Today's youth rely on their computers and cell phones to do assignments, record numbers, and save important information. As a result, young people can find themselves unprepared in an emergency, such as an electrical blackout. If their computer and phone batteries die, these young people will be lost.

Supporting Example

For example, I do all my schoolwork on my computer. When my computer crashed last week, I lost my only draft of an essay that was due the next day. As a result, I got a bad grade.

Exercise 6 Identifying topic sentences and supporting sentences

For each set of sentences, write *TS* next to the topic sentence. Write *SS* next to the supporting sentences.

1. SS a. Mosquitoes are attracted to heat.
   SS b. Mosquitoes will fly several miles to find food.
   SS c. Only the female mosquito bites.
   TS d. Mosquitoes are interesting insects.
   SS e. Mosquitoes have poor eye-sight but use heat to find blood.

2. ____ a. The first type of hotel is an airport hotel.
   ____ b. Many airport hotel guests are passengers whose flights were delayed or cancelled.
   ____ c. There are two types of hotels in most major cities.
   ____ d. The second type of hotel is a downtown hotel.
   ____ e. Guests of downtown hotels include tourists and business people.

3. ____ a. Part-time jobs teach students skills they need for the future.
   ____ b. They also learn about job responsibilities.
   ____ c. Students learn how to be on time.
   ____ d. They learn about working with others.
   ____ e. Students learn about business.

4. ____ a. The collection includes music from Spain, Ethiopia, and Egypt.
   ____ b. I also enjoy going to concerts by musicians from different countries.
   ____ c. Last month I went to a concert by a famous musician from Korea.
   ____ d. I have a large collection of world music on my MP3 player.
   ____ e. One of my hobbies is listening to international music.

5. ____ a. If uniforms are required, students will not wear T-shirts with offensive messages.
   ____ b. Uniforms prevent students from wearing improper clothing.
   ____ c. All high schools should require their students to wear uniforms.
   ____ d. Students who wear uniforms do not have to worry about the latest fashions.
   ____ e. Students do not need to worry about matching colors or styles.

Rhetorical Focus

The Concluding Sentence

The concluding, or final, sentence of a paragraph usually reminds the reader of the topic and controlling idea. The concluding sentence restates the main idea.

Topic Sentence: I love the color red because it is a symbol of strength.

Concluding Sentence: I like to live life in a strong way, so I think I will always admire the color red.

In addition to restating the main idea, the concluding sentence may:

- warn the reader.
  If you do not follow these steps, you may not get the grade that you want.
- make a prediction.
  Soon everyone will be driving pollution-free cars.
- give an opinion about the topic.
  Some people might disagree, but I think lamb is the best meat for grilling.

Sometimes writers signal the concluding sentence with the phrase *In conclusion*.

In conclusion, learning a second language has many advantages.

Exercise 7 Identifying concluding sentences

Read each topic sentence. Then check (✓) the sentence that would make the best conclusion.

1. There are four steps to finding a cheap airline ticket online.
   _____ a. Airline tickets will be more expensive in the future.
   __✓__ b. Following these steps will help you find the best price.
   _____ c. Everybody wants to save money on airline tickets.
2. Video games can benefit children.
   _____ a. Some video games teach children decision-making strategies.
   _____ b. In addition to playing video games, watching some educational programs on TV is good for children.
   _____ c. These benefits can have lasting effects on children.
3. The government can encourage people to recycle by taking the following steps.
   _____ a. Without these measures, people are less likely to recycle.
   _____ b. The government should pick up the recycling from people's houses at least once a week.
   _____ c. The government should do more to protect the environment.

Exercise 8 Examining concluding sentences

Circle the word that best describes each of the concluding sentences.

1. If you follow these steps, you will never lose your keys again.
   a. prediction   b. opinion   c. warning
2. Students who are not careful with credit cards can go into debt quickly.
   a. prediction   b. opinion   c. warning
3. Antlaya, Turkey is one of the most beautiful cities in the world.
   a. prediction   b. opinion   c. warning
4. You will be able to fold a beautiful paper crane with only a little practice.
   a. prediction   b. opinion   c. warning
5. The desert is a beautiful but dangerous place to hike, so do your research, and prepare carefully.
   a. prediction   b. opinion   c. warning

In **Writing Process Part 3** you will . . .

- learn about unity in paragraphs.
- learn how to create coherence in your writing.

Writing Process Part 3 | Unity and Coherence

Good academic writers follow specific steps to make sure that their writing is both clear and accurate. These writers gather, organize, and develop ideas. They write two or more drafts. When they revise each draft, good writers look for unity, coherence, and grammatical mistakes. They correct these mistakes to develop their final drafts.

Rhetorical Focus

Unity Within a Paragraph

A paragraph must have **unity.** A paragraph has unity when all the sentences support a single idea.

- The topic sentence must have only one controlling idea. Additional controlling ideas make the paragraph lose its focus.
- The supporting sentences in a paragraph must support or explain the controlling idea. Their examples, details, steps, or definitions must all support the same idea. Ideas that do not support the topic sentence cause the paragraph to lose its focus.
- The concluding sentence usually restates the idea in the topic sentence. However, it should use different words. It can give an additional thought, but it must not introduce a new topic.

Topic Sentence

My friend Adriana is generous.

Supporting Sentences

She often lets travelers stay in her home. She hosts many students when they go to her home for study groups or dinners. She sends money to her family in Chile every month to help them with their bills. She often brings flowers or other gifts to her friends on their birthdays. She also takes food to older people who are sick or lonely.

Concluding Sentence

Adriana is one of the most generous people I know.

Note that all the sentences are about Adriana's generosity. A sentence about the way she looks or about her job will not support the unity of the paragraph unless it somehow relates to Adriana's generosity.

Exercise 1 Reading a student paragraph

Read the paragraph. Where did the pink sheep come from?

The Pink Sheep

Many years ago, a special gift came to me in an interesting way. When I was a small boy, I enjoyed playing in my yard. One day, I found a hole in the wall of my yard. It was near the ground, so I could not see through the hole, but I knew that behind the wall was my neighbor's yard. I wanted to see that yard, so I used rocks to make the hole wider. One day, when I was trying to break through the wall, a small hand appeared from the hole. The hand was holding a rubber sheep. The sheep was pink, and it had wide eyes. I took the rubber sheep. Then I pushed my favorite wooden truck through the hole to give to the child on the other side. I bought the truck with money I received for the New Year. Years later, when I was old enough to go out by myself, I went around the corner to find the child who gave me that special gift, but nobody was in that house. Another neighbor said that a girl used to live there and that she was the same age as I was. I never found her, but her gift still has a special meaning for me.

Exercise 2 Examining the student paragraph

Respond to the questions and statements below.

1. Circle the topic and underline the controlling idea.
2. After you read the topic sentence, what did you expect the supporting ideas to explain? Write your answer in your own words.

   ____

   ____

3. One sentence in the paragraph is off-topic. It does not support the unity of the paragraph. Draw a line through it.
4. What other supporting sentences would you add to the paragraph?

   ____

   ____

Exercise 3 Recognizing unity in supporting sentences

Read the following topic sentences. Underline the controlling idea in each topic sentence. Then check (✓) each sentence that supports the topic sentence.

1. I am an organized person.
   ✓ a. My desk is always neat and tidy.
   ✓ b. I have a system for organizing my papers, and I can always find what I need.
   ____ c. I feel uncomfortable when I am in a strange place.
   ✓ d. My friends always want me to help them put their closets in order.
2. Twenty Questions is an easy game to play when you are traveling.
   ____ a. One person must think of a person, place, or object.
   ____ b. Sometimes people travel by car and sometimes by train or airplane.
   ____ c. It is very important to travel with people that you get along with.
   ____ d. The other players take turns asking questions that can only be answered "yes" or "no."
3. Tea and coffee are very different from each other.
   ____ a. Coffee has more caffeine than tea does.
   ____ b. Coffee and tea both have caffeine.
   ____ c. People enjoy tea and coffee during social events.
   ____ d. Tea is much more common around the world than coffee is.
4. People should not buy expensive cars.
   ____ a. Some people spend a fourth of their income on a car payment, which is unnecessary.
   ____ b. Cars do not increase in value, so they are not good investments.
   ____ c. Car companies are always looking for ways to make cars safer on the road.
   ____ d. People who do not pay cash must also pay interest, so they lose even more money when they buy an expensive car.
5. It is easy to get a sports injury.
   ____ a. Many people enjoy sports.
   ____ b. Runners often have problems with their ankles and knees.
   ____ c. Basketball players can break their fingers or get knocked over by other players.
   ____ d. Many people join gyms but never go there to exercise.

6. My city is famous because of its architecture.
   _____ a. We have old red-tiled buildings around the main square.
   _____ b. The restaurants near the beach are famous for their great lobster.
   _____ c. The city has tree-lined boulevards with beautiful limestone buildings and bronze statues.
   _____ d. A famous university is located on the side of a mountain and can be seen from all over the city.

Exercise 4 Editing for unity

Read the paragraph below, and find the three sentences that do not relate to the controlling idea. Cross them out.

Life in a New Place

Thai people living in Dallas, Texas, must make many adjustments to be like Texans. First of all, they must learn to eat many new kinds of food. For example, Texans eat hamburgers and pizza because these foods are inexpensive and easy to find. However, most Thai people like spicy dishes made with green or red curry. In addition, in Dallas, Thai people can meet people from other countries who have many different cultures and languages. For example, more than 30 percent of the population in Dallas is Mexican. Another 2 percent of the population is Vietnamese. More than 5 percent of Dallas's population is originally from Pakistan. Pakistan is also an interesting country to visit. The weather in Dallas requires another kind of adjustment. Like Thailand, Dallas has many months of hot weather, but Dallas is not as humid as Thailand. However, Dallas also has cold winters, which are strange for Thai people. Sometimes it even snows in Dallas. I never saw snow in Thailand. Before I came to the United States, I had worked in a bank. There are banks in Dallas, too. Although life is different in Texas, most Thai people find Dallas to be an interesting and exciting place to live.

Exercise 5 Developing unity

Write two supporting sentences for each of the following topic sentences. Then exchange books with a partner, and check your partner's sentences for unity.

1. Computers are useful in many ways.

   They are great for doing research on the Web. ____________

   Students can use computers for writing research papers. ____________

2. Good restaurants have certain important characteristics.

   ____

   ____

3. People in my country always eat a healthy breakfast.

   ____

   ____

4. There are activities in a park for family members of all ages.

   ____

   ____

5. There are many ways to show respect to older people.

   ____

   ____

6. When you go camping, there are some things you should take with you.

   ____

   ____

Rhetorical Focus

Coherence Within a Paragraph

In addition to unity, a paragraph must also have **coherence.** This means that the supporting details are organized in a logical way.

Writers often use **time**, **space**, or **order of importance** to present the supporting information in a paragraph coherently. The following example is organized by space.

> When you are close to the airport, you will see many signs for the different terminals. After you pass the signs, you will drive over a hill. The airport is on the other side of the hill. On your right, you will see the international terminal. This terminal is two stories tall. The front is all glass. On the left, you will see the domestic terminals.

Exercise 6 Identifying patterns of coherence

Read the paragraphs below. Then circle the word that best describes the paragraph's organization.

Paragraph 1

My favorite restaurant is in an old house. It is very convenient for my family to go there because it is in my neighborhood. We can drive, or if the evening is pleasant, we can walk there. It has a nice atmosphere and friendly service. We know some of the waiters and waitresses. We enjoy talking to them because they ask us about our children. We especially like the decorations. The walls are soft yellow, and fresh flowers sit on the tables. Finally, the food is excellent. The cook is the owner, and he makes delicious dishes with fresh ingredients. We always enjoy our meals at this great restaurant.

Time	Space	Order of Importance

Paragraph 2

My favorite restaurant is in an old house. My husband and I enjoy eating there on summer evenings. We usually walk from our house so we can enjoy our neighbors' gardens and get a little bit of exercise. The afternoon sun shines through the trees, but it is not too bright. We arrive at dusk. If we are lucky, we can sit outside. The waiter brings a basket of warm bread and cold drinks. We have an appetizer or a salad while the sun goes down. Then the waiter lights the candles while we enjoy the main course. By the time we finish dessert, it is nighttime. We walk home slowly, feeling full but happy in the moonlight.

Time	Space	Order of Importance

Exercise 7 Evaluating coherence within a paragraph

Read the following paragraphs. Which one has better coherence? What is the pattern of organization?

Paragraph 1

Soccer brings the world together in many ways. During the World Cup, people watch from all over the world. If they cannot see the game in person, they watch it on television. Many countries participate in the World Cup. People learn about the teams from different countries, and they learn something about those countries. When people watch the World Cup, they do not care if the game is on at 4:00 a.m. in their country. They will stay up to watch it. They learn about the flags from different countries because they see the fans waving the flags.

Paragraph 2

The best way to meet new friends is to take a class. First, all the people in a class have something in common. They all want to learn about the subject, so there is something to talk about. Second, everyone sees each other every time the class meets, so there are many opportunities to get to know others. Third, there are often activities and group projects, so students can work together. This is the best way to get to know people. By the end of the class, it is hard not to know your classmates.

In **Writing Process Part 4** you will . . .

- learn about simple sentence structure.
- learn about end punctuation and capitalization.
- learn about fragments and run-on sentences.

Writing Process Part 4 | Editing Your Writing

When you edit, you make changes that will improve your writing and correct mistakes.

Language and Grammar Focus

Simple Sentence Structure

A **sentence** is a statement that expresses a complete idea. Sentences form the building blocks of written communication. They include affirmative statements, negative statements, and questions. A complete sentence must have a **subject** and a **verb**.

Subject

A subject tells who or what the sentence is about.
A subject can be a name.

> **Emily** smiled.

A subject can be a noun or a pronoun.

> **My teacher** loves her job. **She** smiled.

A subject can be singular or plural.

> **Exercise** is the key to good health. **Chairs** come in many forms.

A subject can be more than one word.

> **Yoko and Hiro** have eight children.

Verb

The verb refers to an action or a state. It shows tense or time. Two common tenses are simple present and simple past.

> Omar **sings**. *(simple present)*
> The ducks **walked** across the street. *(simple past)*

A sentence can have more than one verb.

> My brother **studied** hard and **earned** a degree in economics.

Exercise 1 Identifying subjects and verbs

Underline the subject, and circle the verb(s) in each sentence.

1. My mother raised seven children.
2. She cooked and cleaned all day long.
3. My father and his brother have a small business.
4. Many bookstores in the United States offer free WiFi.
5. Indira Gandhi was prime minster of India for a total of 15 years.

Exercise 2 Writing simple sentences

Answer each question below in a complete sentence. Then exchange books with a partner. Underline the subject and circle the verb in your partner's sentences.

1. Where is Cairo?

   Cairo is the capital of Egypt.

2. What sports are popular in your country?

   ____

3. What city is the best place to live?

   ____

4. How much did your textbook cost?

   ____

5. When did your parents marry?

   ____

6. How often does your class meet?

   ____

Language and Grammar Focus

Punctuation and Capitalization

The first word in a sentence is always **capitalized.**

> **T**he wedding lasts for several days.

A complete sentence usually ends in a **period.**

> A good speech begins with a joke**.**

A question ends with a **question mark.**

> Do you enjoy learning about the world**?**

Sometimes, writers use an **exclamation mark** to give emphasis to a sentence.

> I looked down, and sliding across my bare foot was a giant green snake**!**

Exercise 3 Using correct punctuation and capitalization

Add the correct punctuation and capitalization to the following sentences.

1. How did Mao Tse-tung change people's lives in China
2. we gathered in the Zocalo to celebrate mexico's independence
3. what is the best time of year to visit Sydney, Australia
4. I had never dreamed that glaciers would be so beautiful

Exercise 4 Identifying subjects, verbs, and end punctuation

Read the paragraph. In each sentence, underline the subject and circle the verb(s). Then draw a box around the end punctuation.

Summary by the Sea

My favorite memory is about a summer trip. It happened a long time ago before my brothers got married and moved out. My parents had seven children. All seven of us piled into one car for a summer vacation by the beach. We traveled in that crowded car for two days! Finally we arrived at a small house near the beach. It had one big room with many beds and another room for eating and cooking. The kids spent all day outside. We played together in the water. Sometimes my mother made a picnic dinner. We sat on the sand to eat and watch the sun go down. One night we brought out blankets and slept by the water. We talked and looked at the stars until late at night. The sand was comfortable to sleep on. I molded the sand around my body to get a better sleeping position. It was wonderful to wake up to the sound of waves and the smell of the ocean. This wonderful summer vacation was the best experience of my life.

Language and Grammar Focus

Fragments

Every sentence must have a subject and a verb. Sentences must also express complete ideas. A sentence that is missing a subject or a verb is incomplete. It is called a **fragment**.

Incorrect Sentences

x I like Singapore because is a clean city. *(subject is missing* after *because)*

x They successful. *(verb is missing)*

Correct Sentences

I like Singapore because **it** is a clean city.

They **are** successful.

Exercise 5 Identifying and correcting fragments

Decide whether each fragment below is missing a subject or a verb. Then rewrite it correctly.

1. Some food very spicy. Some food is very spicy.
2. Corn my favorite vegetable. ______
3. Is very bright in the afternoon. ______
4. In the afternoon takes a two-hour nap. ______

Language and Grammar Focus

Run-on Sentences

Two sentences that run together without correct punctuation are called **run-on sentences**. One way to correct a run-on sentence is to put a period between the sentences. Another way is to add a **comma** and a connecting word such as *and, but,* or *so.*

x I received a letter it was from my sister. (INCORRECT: no punctuation between two sentences)

I received a letter**.** It was from my sister. (CORRECT: period added between the sentences)

x They laughed, I felt better. (INCORRECT: comma alone between two sentences)

They laughed, **and** I felt better. (CORRECT: connecting word added)

Exercise 6 Correcting run-on sentences

Correct the following run-on sentences by rewriting them.

1. I am a full-time student, I live in a great apartment near campus.
   I am a full-time student, and I live in a great apartment near campus.
2. There are mice living underneath my house they make a lot of noise at night.
   ______
3. I used to eat rice and vegetables for breakfast now I eat cereal and milk.
   ______
4. Reading helps you learn new vocabulary, it also improves your grammar.
   ______

Exercise 7 Editing for fragments and run-on sentences

Read and edit the paragraph. There are two more fragment mistakes and three run-on mistakes. Use appropriate punctuation and capitalization.

Working as a Hotel Receptionist

Being a part-time receptionist in a hotel provides many useful work skills for young people. First, young people can learn about working with the public. Hotel receptionists have to interact with guests every day, they also answer phone calls and make reservations. In addition, because there travelers from a lot of different countries, hotel receptionists learn how to interact with people from different language and cultural backgrounds. They need to learn English, it is the language that most international travelers are able to speak. They also learn about other cultures. Which is a useful skill for a lot of international jobs in the future. Finally, hotel receptionists have to deal with the guests' complaints, they learn problem-solving skills. In conclusion, a part-time hotel receptionist job gives a young person a variety of skills to use in the future.

In **Review** you will . . .

- review the elements of a paragraph.
- review end punctuation.
- practice correcting fragments and run-on sentences.

In Putting It All Together, you will review what you learned in this unit.

Exercise 1 Identifying the elements of a paragraph

Use the words in the box to label the formatting elements of the paragraph.

a. margin	b. double-spacing	c. indent	d. title

____ 1.

____ 2.

____ 3.

____ 4.

My Grandfather the Baker

My grandfather has a lot of respect in our community. He is the owner of a bakery called The Bread Factory. Baking has been his profession since he was young. He started working in the bakery at the age of 13. He learned many recipes. The most delicious and secret recipe uses oatmeal and other ingredients that only he knows. This bread made him famous. Nowadays, he makes some bread only once in a while because he gets tired easily. Instead, he sits at a table, and the people of the town come to buy bread. Everyone admires my grandfather because he is an honest and hardworking man.

Exercise 2 Identifying topic sentences and supporting sentences

For each set of sentences, write *TS* next to the topic sentence. Write *SS* next to the supporting sentences.

1. ____ a. The calendars are different.
   ____ b. The weekend starts on Friday instead of Saturday.
   ____ c. My country does not follow Greenwich time.
   ____ d. There are some very specific differences between my part of the world and western countries.

2. ____ a. I was traveling to Jakarta, Indonesia to visit my cousin.
   ____ b. My plane was delayed, so I was stuck at the airport.
   ____ c. I experienced a strange coincidence last year.
   ____ d. I heard my math teacher from my old hometown calling my name.

3. _____ a. I like several things about my English class.

_____ b. I meet many new friends from different countries.

_____ c. Every day, I learn new words, and I keep them in a notebook.

_____ d. Sometimes we play games and laugh during class time.

4. _____ a. You can use the Internet to find information, but if you do not have the right skills, you can waste a lot of time.

_____ b. The Internet can be incredibly useful if you know how to use it.

_____ c. There are opportunities to buy and sell products on the Internet, but you have to know the proper way to send money.

_____ d. The Internet is a good place to find a job.

Exercise 3 Evaluating concluding sentences

Read the paragraphs below. Then read the concluding sentences that follow, and decide which one works best. Copy the sentence you choose into the paragraph.

There They Are!

I feel happy whenever I am at a train station waiting for someone who is close to me. I was the youngest child in my family, so my older brothers and sisters left home before I did. However, they always returned for vacations and holidays. My mother, father, and I were always at the train station to greet them. I enjoyed the smell of the train and the roaring noise it made as the big black engine pulled into the station. I would jump up and down trying to see while everyone crowded around the doors. "There they are!" my mother would cry. I would run to jump into the arms of my beloved brother or sister.

____

____

a. In conclusion, I always had an enjoyable visit with my brothers and sisters.
b. In conclusion, my whole family likes train stations.
c. Now I am an adult, but I still feel joy when I go to the train station to meet someone I love.

A Wise Shopper

A consumer can save a lot of money by shopping wisely. This means he is always looking for sales and collecting coupons. It also means that the person is not a compulsive shopper. In other words, the wise consumer does his research and makes a plan so that he knows what he is looking for. He is not tempted by attractive products that are not necessary. Sometimes he goes home without purchasing anything. He might think he wasted his time, but he knows he did not waste his money. ______________________________

____

a. In conclusion, a compulsive shopper can never be a wise shopper.
b. In conclusion, a wise shopper also keeps a budget so that he knows how much he can spend.
c. In conclusion, a wise shopper finds ways to save money on the price and to avoid buying what he does not need.

Exercise 4 Editing a paragraph

Read and edit the paragraph. Fix run-on sentences, fragments, and mistakes in capitalization. There are three sentences that do not support the topic sentence. Cross them out.

My Red Couch

I acquired a couch in an interesting way. I was walking to the bus stop and I saw the couch on the sidewalk. There was a sign on the couch that read "I am free. Take me home." I like taking the bus to school because I can study on the bus or read the newspaper. I really liked the couch. It had a beautiful wooden frame and red fabric. However, there was a problem. I did not have a truck my apartment was five blocks away. suddenly, I saw my classmate across the street. She usually sat next to me in a computer class. I told her my problem, she offered to help. It a big, heavy couch, but my friend and I carried it down the street. When we got tired, we sat down to rest on the couch. Finally, we brought it to my door, and my neighbor helped carry it upstairs. My neighbor works in a department store. It was a funny day for me, and I like to remember this day whenever I come home and see my beautiful red couch.

Exercise 5 Identifying subjects and verbs

Underline the subject, and circle the verb(s) in each sentence.

1. Many children like hot chocolate in the morning.
2. They do not like coffee.
3. India has over one billion people.
4. Eva Perón was the first lady of Argentina from 1946 to 1952.
5. On July 20, 1969, Neil Armstrong became the first human to step on the moon.
6. Lions and tigers are two examples of wild animals.

Exercise 6 Using end punctuation

Add the correct end punctuation to the following sentences.

1. How do airplanes stay in the sky
2. When I got home, there were candles and fresh flowers everywhere
3. He was late to his own birthday dinner
4. The guests were very happy with the food
5. Which countries have the best beaches for surfing

Exercise 7 Identifying and correcting fragments

Decide whether each fragment below is missing a subject or a verb. Then rewrite it correctly. Use a separate piece of paper.

1. Suddenly fell down.
2. I like Hanoi because has a lot of energy.
3. I walking beside the lake with my best friend.
4. My first day in college an exciting day for me.
5. In the morning a lot of traffic on the freeway.
6. The school library located in the student center.

Exercise 8 Identifying and correcting run-on sentences

Correct the following run-on sentences by rewriting them.

1. We watched a movie it was about a little girl who had lost her mother.

   ____

   ____

2. We have a harvest moon festival every year in our city, there are parades and kiosks with noodle soup and other delicious food.

   ____

   ____

3. I reviewed my lessons every day last semester, I passed all my tests with high grades.

   ____

   ____

4. School cafeterias should not serve junk food they should replace it with vegetables and fruit.

   ____

   ____

5. Learning English opens a lot of doors for immigrants for example they can find a job more easily.

   ____

   ____

6. The man woke up in the middle of the night it was dark outside.

   ____

   ____

UNIT 2

Descriptive Paragraphs

Academic Focus | Anthropology

Unit Goals

Rhetorical Focus

- descriptive organization

Language and Grammar Focus

- specific language
- adjectives in descriptive writing
- *be* to define and describe

In a descriptive paragraph, the writer uses words that create an image. The writer helps the reader see, touch, feel, smell, or taste the topic. In this unit, you will write a descriptive paragraph about a special possession.

Exercise 1 Thinking about the topic

Discuss the picture with a partner.

- How is the woman dressed?
- Where is she?
- What do you think she is thinking?
- Do you think this picture was taken long ago or recently? Explain your answer.
- Have you ever seen someone dressed this way? If so, where?

Exercise 2 Reading about the topic

Anthropologists often study objects and their use to learn about cultural beliefs. Prapulla is a young Indian bride. She and her husband, Shekar, are moving to New York. Prapulla must decide how she will dress in her new country. Why is her traditional Indian sari so special to Prapulla?

Sari of the Gods

En route to New York on the **jumbo**, Shekar had discreetly opened up the conversation about what she'd wear once they were in America. At the mention of skirts she had flared up so defiantly he had to leave the seat. For Prapulla, it was not convenience but **convention** that made the difference. She had always **prized** her saris, especially on the occasions when she wore her wedding sari with its blue, **hand-spun silk** and its silver **border** on which images of the gods had been **embroidered**.

. . .

She remembered the day she had shopped for the sari. It had been a week before her wedding. The entire family had gone to the silk **bazaar** and spent the day looking for the perfect one. They had at last found it in the only hand-spun sari shop in the market. The merchant had explained that the weaver who had knitted the gods into its border had died soon after, taking his **craft** with him. This was his last sari, his parting gift to some lucky bride.

Adapted from Chandra, G. S. Sharat *Sari of the Gods*. Minneapolis: Coffee House Press, 1989.

en route: on the way
jumbo: a large airplane
convention: a traditional way of behaving or doing something
prized: considered very valuable
hand-spun: woven by hand
silk: an expensive, soft, smooth fabric
border: the edge of something
embroidered: decorated with small stitches
bazaar: an open market with many shops and stalls
craft: ability or skill

Exercise 3 Understanding the text

Write *T* for true or *F* for false for each statement.

_____ 1. Prapulla went shopping for her wedding sari with her family.

_____ 2. Prapulla's wedding sari was made by hand.

_____ 3. Prapulla's wedding sari was white.

_____ 4. The man who wove Prapulla's wedding sari told her she was lucky.

_____ 5. The sari was the last one in the store.

Exercise 4 Responding to the text

Respond to the questions and statements below.

1. Circle the sentence that describes Prapulla's reaction to the idea of wearing skirts.
2. Underline once the sentence that tells the reader how the wedding sari looked.
3. Underline twice the sentence that tells the reader what was different about the sari shop where Prapulla found her wedding sari.
4. Prapulla and her husband don't agree about how Prapulla should dress in America. Why do you think Prapulla feels strongly about wearing a sari? Why does her husband disagree? ____

   ____
5. Who do you agree with? Why? ____

   ____

Exercise 5 Freewriting

Write for ten minutes in your journal. Choose from topics below or an idea of your own. Express your thoughts and feelings. Don't worry about mistakes.

- Prapulla feels strongly about her wedding sari. Write about a piece of clothing or a possession (something you own) that is special to you.
- Why do people feel more strongly about some possessions than about others?
- What item of clothing represents your culture? How?
- Are connections with possessions important? Why or why not?
- Describe a time when you wanted to do something, but someone else wanted you to do something differently. What happened?

In **Writing Process Step 2** you will . . .

- learn about descriptive organization.
- brainstorm ideas and specific vocabulary to use in your writing.
- determine the audience and purpose for your descriptive paragraph.
- create an outline for your paragraph.

WRITING TASK In this unit, you will write a descriptive paragraph about a special possession. Describe the possession including how it looks and feels. Express your feelings about it. Explain why this possession is meaningful to you. Go to the Web to use the Online Writing Tutor.

Exercise 1 Brainstorming ideas

Think about a special possession that you have. Fill in the ovals below with words or phrases that describe people, places, feelings, and other memories you associate with the possession.

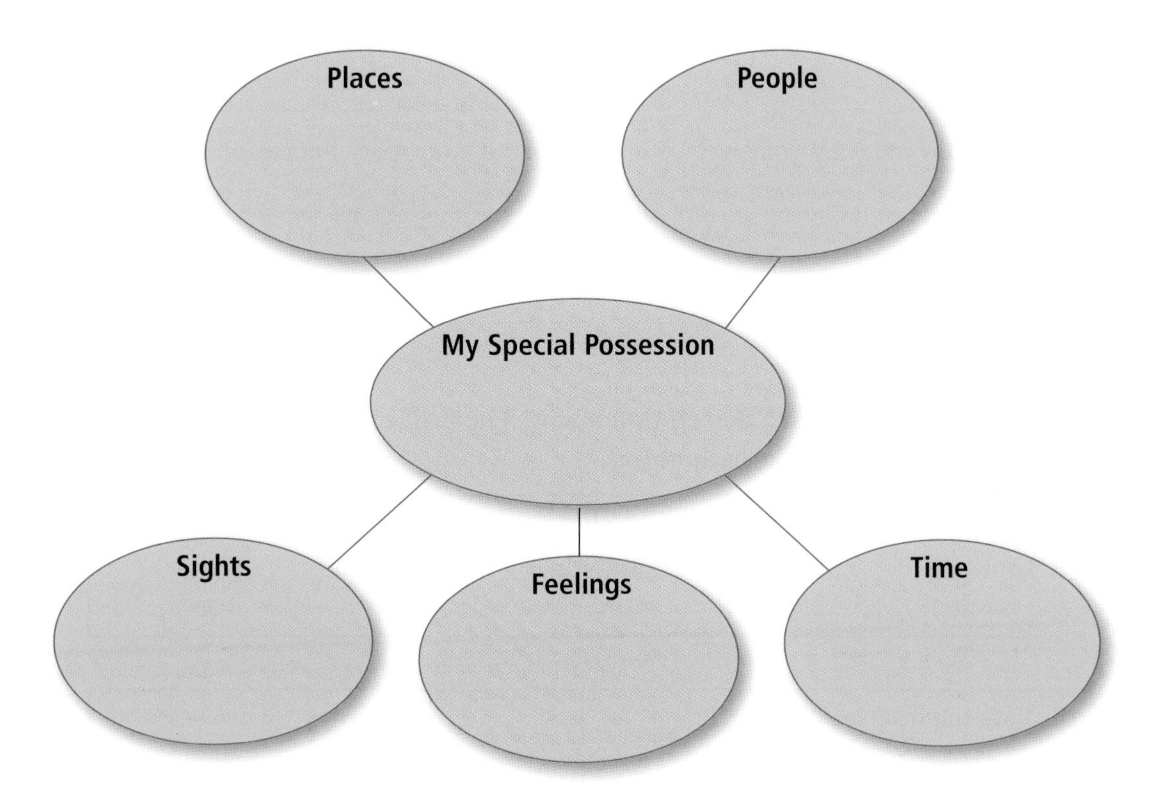

Exercise 2 Identifying audience and purpose

A. Examine the audience and purpose of the reading on page 31. Respond to the questions and statements below.

1. Where would you expect to find this story? (Choose all that apply.)
   a. in a newspaper
   b. in a biography
   c. in a professional magazine
2. What is the purpose of the reading?
   a. to explain how Prapulla got to New York
   b. to describe where Prapulla buys her clothes
   c. to describe Prapulla's saris and why they are important to her

B. Think about your audience (the people who will read your paragraph). Then answer the questions below.

1. How well do your readers know you?

____

____

2. What will your readers need to know about the possession to understand why it is important to you?

____

____

3. What do you want your readers to learn about you?

____

____

4. What do you want your readers to know about your special possession?

____

____

Exercise 3 Brainstorming vocabulary

Write an object for each description below. Then fill in the chart with adjectives from the box to describe each object.

plastic	metal	wood	silk	ceramic
antique	sleek	hand made	elaborate	simple
smooth	rough	soft	sharp	heavy

1. an important cultural item ____________________	
2. a useful tool ____________________	
3. a family treasure ____________________	
4. an electronic device ____________________	
5. a well-loved toy ____________________	

Rhetorical Focus

Descriptive Organization

A **descriptive paragraph** describes a person, place, or thing so that readers can almost see it in their minds.

Topic Sentence

- The topic sentence in a descriptive paragraph introduces the item that the writer will describe.
- It may also include the writer's general feeling or opinion about the item.

Supporting Sentences

- The supporting sentences give background information about the item.
- The supporting sentences also give details to describe how the item looks, smells, feels, sounds, or tastes.
- The supporting sentences may also describe how the writer feels about the item.

Concluding Sentence

- The paragraph ends with a concluding sentence. It restates the idea in the topic sentence using different words.

Exercise 4 Reading a student paragraph

Read the paragraph. What does the writer plan to do with the car?

The Long Life of My Grandfather's Car

I own a car that has special meaning for me because it belonged to my grandfather. When he was a young man, he saved money so he could buy a beautiful car to use on trips around the country. He bought a Cadillac convertible. It was white and blue with silver trim. There were white circles on the tires. The car had a powerful horn that made people jump out of my grandfather's way. The seats were also white, but the dashboard was black. The steering wheel had a brown leather cover. The mats were gray and always clean. My grandfather took very good care of his car. After my grandfather died, my uncle gave the car to me. I am very happy because the car still has the original motor, and the body is intact. If it has problems, I will fix it myself. I plan to take very good care of my grandfather's car. Someday I will use it to travel to all the states and cities that my grandfather visited when he was a young man.

Exercise 5 Examining the student paragraph

A. Answer the following questions about the student paragraph.

1. Which of the following sentences best describes the main idea of the paragraph?
   a. The writer's grandfather traveled around the country in the 1950s.
   b. The writer likes Cadillac convertibles.
   c. The writer has strong feelings about his grandfather's car.
   d. The writer will take good care of the car.
2. Which two of the following types of details did the author include in the paragraph?
   a. appearance
   b. smell
   c. sound
   d. feel
3. Why is the car important to the writer?
   a. It connects the writer to his grandfather.
   b. The writer likes old cars.
   c. The writer likes to work on cars and repair engines.
   d. The writer wants to travel around the country.

B. Examine the organization of the paragraph. Respond to the questions and statements below. Compare your answers with a partner.

1. Underline the topic sentence in the paragraph twice.
2. Write the supporting sentence that tells why the writer's grandfather bought the car.

   ____

   ____

3. Underline two supporting sentences that tell what the car looks like.
4. Circle the phrases that tell how the car has been cared for.
5. This writer frequently uses colors to describe what different parts of the car look like. Read the paragraph again and write the color of each part of the car.

   trim ____

   circles on the tires ____

   seats ____

   dashboard ____

   mats ____

   steering wheel cover ____

Exercise 6 Completing an outline

Look back at the paragraph on page 35. Then write the missing information into the outline below.

Topic Sentence

Item the author describes: *a Cadillac convertible car*

The author's general feeling about the item: ______________________

____

____

Supporting Sentences

Background information about the item: ______________________

____

____

Descriptive details about the item: ______________________

____

____

Details about the author's feelings: ______________________

____

____

Concluding Sentence

Restated idea: ______________________

____

Exercise 7 Writing an outline

Review your brainstorming ideas and the information on organizing a descriptive paragraph. Then go to the Web to print out an outline template for your paragraph.

In **Writing Process Step 3** you will . . .

- learn to use specific language in your writing.
- write a first draft of your descriptive paragraph.

Exercise 1 Reading a student paragraph

Read the paragraph. How does the author feel about the abacus?

An Abacus

I have an ancient abacus from my mother's village. In the old days, people used them for business, and children used them to learn math. My abacus has a wooden frame, beads, and ten metal bars. The beads slide across the bar. The first row shows the numbers 1 to 10. The second row shows the numbers 11 to 20, and the third row shows the numbers 21 to 30. The rows continue to 100. The beads along each row are a separate color to make it easier to understand the numbers. The round beads click as they hit each other. One, click, two, click, three, click. Each click puts emphasis on the numbers counted. It is more advanced than just counting on fingers. Now my children use a calculator. Calculators are faster, but they only show a number on a screen. With an abacus, my children touch the beads and can see why the answer is correct.

Exercise 2 Examining the student paragraph

A. Respond to the questions and statements about the student paragraph.

1. What does an abacus do? ______________________________

____

2. Have you ever seen or used an abacus? Describe your experience.

____

____

3. What do you think children should use: a calculator or an abacus? Why?

____

____

B. Examine the organization of the paragraph. Respond to the questions and statements below.

1. Underline the topic sentence.
2. Which sentence explains the order of description in the paragraph?
   a. First the writer describes who used an abacus. Then she describes what the abacus sounds and looks like. She concludes by telling about her own abacus.
   b. First the writer introduces the abacus. Then she tells what the abacus looks like. Then she describes what it sounds like. Finally, she concludes by telling why an abacus can help a child learn through touch and seeing.
   c. First the writer describes what an abacus is used for. Then she describes who uses abacuses. Finally she concludes by telling how the calculator has replaced the abacus.
   d. First the writer describes what an abacus is used for. Then she explains that the computer has replaced the abacus. She concludes by telling how useful the abacus is.
3. Write some of the words and phrases that the writer uses to describe the abacus.
   - how the abacus looks ______________________________

     ____
   - how the abacus sounds ______________________________

     ____
   - other descriptive words/phrases ______________________________

     ____

Language and Grammar Focus

Using Specific Language

Using **specific language** in descriptive writing helps give the reader a clear image of what something looks, feels, sounds, tastes, or smells like. Read the following examples. Which set of sentences provides a clearer picture?

General Sentences	Sentences with Specific Language
He bought a car.	He bought a shiny, new sportscar.
We heard a noise.	We heard the sound of breaking glass.
Suddenly, I smelled food.	Suddenly, I smelled steak and onions.

In the first column, the words are general. They could be used to describe a variety of cars, noises, or food. In the second column, the writer has replaced the general terms with more specific words. These changes make the topic specific and clearer for the reader.

Exercise 3 Identifying specific language

Read the following pairs of sentences. Put a check (✓) next to the sentence that is more specific.

1. _____ a. I like to wear my grandmother's jewelry.
   __✓__ b. I like to wear my grandmother's pearl necklace.
2. _____ a. My best friend gave me a novel by Chang-Rae Lee.
   _____ b. My best friend gave me a book.
3. _____ a. Someone lent her an umbrella.
   _____ b. Her father lent her a large umbrella.
4. _____ a. I inherited some furniture.
   _____ b. I inherited my grandmother's rocking chair.
5. _____ a. Hassan has a new widescreen laptop.
   _____ b. Hassan has a new computer.

Exercise 4 Adding specific details

Rewrite the following sentences. Replace the underlined words and phrases with words that are more specific.

1. I bought <u>a pair of shoes</u>.
   I bought a pair of running shoes.
2. Maria found <u>some jewelry</u> in the basement.
   ____
3. My mother gave me <u>some money</u>.
   ____
4. I like <u>my desk</u>.
   ____
5. My father enjoyed making <u>things</u>.
   ____
6. My grandparents collected <u>souvenirs</u>.
   ____
7. We always have <u>vegetables</u> with dinner.
   ____

Exercise 5 Editing a paragraph for specific language

A. Read the following paragraph. Underline five more words or phrases that could be more specific. For each underlined word or phrase, write one question that you could ask the writer to help her be more specific.

My Lost Treasure Box

When I left my home town, my relative gave me a special box. She said I could use the box to keep my treasures. The box was made of a special material, and it was painted a bright color. When I opened it, it played a pretty song. I kept this box on my dresser, and I used it to store my things. Unfortunately, I lost my beautiful box when I moved to a different city. I will always remember the box and the relative who gave it to me.

1. What town did you come from?
2. ______________________________
3. ______________________________
4. ______________________________
5. ______________________________
6. ______________________________

B. Rewrite the paragraph. Change the underlined words and phrases to make them more specific. Compare your paragraph with a partner.

____

____

____

____

____

____

____

____

____

____

Exercise 6 Writing a first draft

GO ONLINE

Review your outline. Then write the first draft of your descriptive paragraph about a possession that is important to you. Go to the Web to use the Online Writing Tutor.

Exercise 7 Peer editing a first draft

A. After writing a first draft, it is helpful to get feedback on your ideas. Exchange paragraphs with two other people. For each paragraph you read, answer the Peer Editor's Questions on a separate piece of paper. Then discuss your responses.

GO ONLINE

Peer Editor's Questions

1. What do you like most about the paragraph?
2. What possession is the paragraph about?
3. What details does the writer provide to help you imagine how the possession looks, feels, sounds, tastes, or smells?
4. What memories does the writer associate with the possession?
5. Why is the possession important to the writer?
6. Where does the paragraph need more details?

Go to the Web to print out a peer editor's worksheet.

B. Review your feedback and the organization guidelines on page 35. Make notes for your revision. In this step, you may add, remove, or rewrite information to clarify your ideas.

In **Writing Process Step 4** you will . . .

- learn to use adjectives in descriptive writing.
- learn to use the verb *be* to describe and define.
- edit your first draft and write a final draft.

Now that you have written a first draft, it is time to edit. When you edit, you make changes that will improve your writing and correct mistakes.

Language and Grammar Focus

GO ONLINE

Using Adjectives in Descriptive Writing

Adjectives are words that describe nouns. Writers use adjectives to give the reader a more complete picture of the people, places, and things they want to describe. Compare the following pairs of phrases. Notice how the adjectives help you "see" the object.

a bicycle — a **racing** bicycle

a desk — a **large**, **metal** desk

An adjective often comes before a noun. If the noun is singular, use *a*, *an*, or *the* before the adjective.

I own **an antique** violin.
My mother gave me **a big** hug.

Adjectives have only one form. Use the same adjective with singular and plural nouns.

a **lovely** bracelet
two **lovely** bracelets

An adjective can come after *be*. When two adjectives come after *be*, separate them with *and*.

These shoes are **comfortable.**
My father's expression is **wise and serious**.

Nouns can also function as adjectives. In the following examples, the first noun describes the second noun.

a **rose** garden
a **pocket** knife

> **!** When a noun functions as an adjective, it is always singular.
>
> two **kitchen** tables
>
> X two kitchens tables (INCORRECT)

Exercise 1 Identifying adjectives

Underline the adjectives in the following sentences.

1. I take care of my <u>sturdy</u>, <u>old</u> bicycle.
2. I am fond of my house plant.
3. It has broad, green leaves and delicate, white flowers.
4. I bought a straw hat at a music festival.
5. It was not expensive, but I liked it because it was practical and attractive.
6. I bought my mug at a small tourist shop at the Lima airport.
7. We planted a vegetable garden behind the house.
8. Friendly people are usually happy.
9. She has a different idea.
10. My favorite books are historical novels.

Exercise 2 Using adjectives

Add two or three adjectives to each sentence to improve the description.

1. My umbrella is like a friend.

   My big, black umbrella is like an old friend.
2. I love my bicycle.

   ____
3. No one understands why I still wear my jeans.

   ____
4. If I could only save one thing from a fire, it would be my chair.

   ____
5. The piano in my parents' house is located in the room.

   ____
6. My mother gave me her ring.

   ____
7. I have a plant and a cat.

   ____
8. There is a tree next to the house.

   ____

Language and Grammar Focus

Using *Be* to Describe and to Define

Use the verb *be* to describe the subject of a sentence. You can use either a noun or an adjective after *be*.

You can use *be* + adjective to describe conditions, physical characteristics, age, and personality.

Condition	Physical Characteristic	Age	Personality
He **is** ready.	I **am** strong.	My daughter **is** six.	Gabriela **is** gracious.

You can use *be* + noun (or noun phrase) to identify or define something. You can also use it to describe occupations and relationships.

Identifying Objects	Describing Occupations	Describing Relationships
It **is** a map.	He **is** a waiter.	We **are** classmates.

> **!** In academic writing contractions of the verb *to be* are not acceptable. Use the full forms of the verb in both affirmative and negative sentences.
>
> The marmoset **is** a small mammal.
>
> They **are** not responsible for the research.

***BE* WITH ADJECTIVES**		
SUBJECT	*BE*	ADJECTIVE
I	**am** **am not**	**healthy.**
He She	**is** **is not**	**athletic.**
You We They	**are** **are not**	**young.**

***BE* WITH NOUNS**		
SUBJECT	*BE*	NOUN PHRASE
I	**am** **am not**	**an honest person.**
He She	**is** **is not**	**a photographer.**
You We They	**are** **are not**	**brothers.**

Exercise 3 Using *be* with adjectives

Finish the sentences with a form of the verb *be* and one or more adjectives to describe the following people.

1. My teacher is creative. ______
2. My classmates ______
3. My parents ______
4. My cousins and I ______
5. I ______

Exercise 4 Using *be* with nouns

Finish each sentence below. Make sure there is a noun in your answer.

1. There are books ______ on my desk.
2. My father is ______.
3. Someone who writes novels is ______.
4. There are ______ downtown.
5. Someone who designs houses is ______.

Exercise 5 Editing a paragraph

Read and edit the paragraph. There are four more mistakes with adjectives.

I have a new digital camera, and I am very excited about using it because it has so many ~~features useful~~ useful features. I do not need to spend a lot of time focusing it. It has automatic focus. People do not have to wait a long time for me to take their picture. In addition, its lens is powerful. I can photograph a person and scenery. Both are clear when I print the finals pictures. Another feature allows me to delete pictures blurry. I save a lot of money because I do not have to print uglys pictures. I am very excited about my new camera. It is easy, and I can take interestings pictures with it. I expect to have a lot of fun with it.

Exercise 6 Editing your first draft and rewriting

Review your paragraph for mistakes. Use the checklist below. Then write a final draft. Go to the Web to use the Online Writing Tutor.

Editor's Checklist

Put a check (✓) as appropriate.

CONTENT AND ORGANIZATION

- ○ 1. Does your paragraph have a topic sentence that introduces the item you are describing?
- ○ 2. Did you provide background information about your possession?
- ○ 3. Does your paragraph include supporting sentences that tell the reader how your possession looks, feels, sounds, and smells?
- ○ 4. Did you include a conclusion that restates your main idea?

LANGUAGE

- ○ 5. Did you include adjectives in your sentences to give your reader a more complete picture?
- ○ 6. Did you use adjectives after articles and before nouns?
- ○ 7. Did you use the verb *be* before adjectives and nouns?
- ○ 8. Did you capitalize the first letter of each sentence and use end punctuation?

Go to the Web to print out a peer editor's worksheet.

In **Review** you will . . .

- practice using specific language in writing.
- practice using adjectives and the verb *be* in writing.

In Putting It All Together, you will review what you learned in this unit.

Exercise 1 Using specific language

Rewrite the following sentences. Replace the underlined words and phrases with words that are more specific.

1. I am reading <u>a book</u>.

   ____

2. In the photograph, the person is holding <u>something</u>.

   ____

3. Laura went to <u>Central America</u> for <u>a while</u>.

   ____

4. It is a picture of <u>a monument</u>.

   ____

5. The water flows through <u>a forest</u>.

   ____

6. Our room looked out over <u>some scenery</u>.

   ____

Exercise 2 Using adjectives

Rewrite the following sentences. Add two or three adjectives to each one.

1. My brother owned a car.

   ____

2. My friend has a sister.

   ____

3. The man was a teacher.

   ____

4. This object is actually a computer.

   ____

Exercise 3 Using *be* with adjectives and nouns

Finish the sentences with a form of the verb *be* and adjectives or nouns to describe the following people and places.

1. My parent's home ______________________________

____

2. My neighbors ______________________________

____

3. The buildings in my neighborhood ______________________________

____

4. My best friend ______________________________

____

Exercise 4 Editing a paragraph

Read and edit the paragraph. There are five mistakes with adjectives.

My most valuable possession is a hand-made Persian carpet. My parents gave it to me as a wedding gift right before I married my husband. This carpet is made of wool and silk. It is rectangular, and it has a gold fringe along the borders. The colors of my carpet are mostly dark red on a cream-colored background, but there are also blue and browns designs woven into it. In the center of the carpet, a round medallion is decorated with exquisites lines and curves. The carpet is not thick soft, but it is lovely to look at. I keep it in my living room because it reminds me of my parents wonderful, and the country beautiful where it was made.

In Timed Writing you will . . .

- practice writing with a time limit.

Practice your test-taking skills with the following practice topic. Read the prompt. Then follow the steps below.

> **Write a descriptive paragraph of your favorite place to visit. Where is it? What do you like most about it? What feelings and memories do you associate with the place?**

Step 1 **BRAINSTORMING:** 5 minutes

List interesting places you have visited. Write specific details about each place. Then choose the place you would like to write a descriptive paragraph about.

Step 2 **OUTLINING:** 5 minutes

Fill in the chart with ideas for your description.

Topic Sentence	
Topic and Importance Introduce your place and state why it is special to you.	
Supporting Sentences	
Background Information Explain where the place is and when you visited it.	
Details Provide details that clearly explain the sights, smells, sounds, and feel of the place.	
Details Describe your feelings about the place.	
Concluding Sentence	
Retelling of the Topic Statement Use different words to restate your main idea.	

Step 3 **WRITING:** 25 minutes

Use your brainstorming notes and outline to write your paragraph on a separate piece of paper.

Step 4 **EDITING:** 10 minutes

When you have finished your paragraph, check it for mistakes. Use the checklist below.

GO ONLINE

Editor's Checklist

Put a check (✓) as appropriate.

- ○ 1. Does the paragraph have a topic sentence that introduces the place?
- ○ 2. Did you include background information about the place?
- ○ 3. Did you include descriptive details about how the place looks, smells, sounds, or feels?
- ○ 4. Did you include details about people and memories you have of the place?
- ○ 5. Did you explain why this place is important to you?
- ○ 6. Did you use specific words as part of your description?
- ○ 7. Did you use adjectives as part of your description?
- ○ 8. Are adjectives used correctly?
- ○ 9. Does your concluding sentence use different words to restate the idea in the topic sentence?

Go to the Web to print out a peer editor's worksheet.

Test-Taking Tip

When you are describing something, remember your five senses: sight, sound, touch, smell, and taste. Include sentences about as many of your senses as you can describe.

Topics for Future Writing

Write a descriptive paragraph on one of the following topics.

Art: Describe a famous artist. Give background information about the person and his or her work. What type of work does the artist do? Why is the artist famous?

Engineering: Describe a particular dam or bridge. When was it built? How does it work? Why is it important?

History: Describe a famous historical figure. Where is the person from? Why is the person important? Is the person still living? What are some of the person's accomplishments?

Literature: Describe a character from a book you have read. When and where does the person live? What is his or her personality? How does the person dress and act? Why did you choose this person?

Sociology: Describe a cultural tradition or celebration. Explain the tradition. Where is it celebrated? Who celebrates it? Why is it important?

UNIT 3

Example Paragraphs

Academic Focus | History

Unit Goals

Rhetorical Focus

- example organization
- examples as supporting details

Language and Grammar Focus

- the simple present
- subject-verb agreement

Writers use examples to help readers understand. A good example supports a more general idea with something specific. In this unit, you will write a paragraph that uses examples as supporting details.

Exercise 1 Thinking about the topic

Discuss the pictures with a partner.

- Describe the pictures. What are they? How are they connected?
- The pictures show a group of stars, or a constellation, called Orion. Many cultures identify certain areas of the night sky as specific constellations. In the past, why was it useful to identify different parts of the sky?
- Can you identify any specific stars or constellations in the sky? How did you learn to do so?
- How has what people know about space, planets, and stars changed in the last fifty years?
- Recently, progress has been made in commercial space flights. Have you ever wanted to travel in space? If you had the opportunity, would you go? Why or why not?

Exercise 2 Reading about the topic

Historians often use biographies to tell the story of a historical figure who has remarkable achievements. The following reading describes the work of Galileo Galilei. What were his discoveries?

New Wonders in the Sky

In March 1610, scholars were very excited over a recently published booklet. In his *Starry Messenger,* Galileo Galilei reported sights in the sky never before seen. Three in particular stood out. The moon is not a smoothly polished **sphere**: it is rough and uneven, with mountains, valleys, and **craters**. They cannot be seen by the unaided eye, but Galileo had created a telescope that could magnify them 20 times.

The telescope also revealed many more stars than anyone had ever imagined. Just in the region of the belt and sword of the constellation Orion, Galileo had marked 80 stars. By eye alone one could make out only three stars in the belt, and six in the sword. Wherever he turned his telescope, Galileo saw ten times as many stars as had been known before. The telescope also showed the **Milky Way** to be not just a **hazy** patch, but clusters of many stars. Most **astonishing** of all, Galileo reported four tiny moons around the planet Jupiter.

MacLachlan, James. *Galileo Galilei: First Physicist.* New York: Oxford University Press. 1997.

sphere: a round object
craters: holes formed when a large object, such as a meteor, hits the surface of a planet
Milky Way: the star system in which Earth is located. It appears as a long white (milky) cloud in the night sky
hazy: foggy, not clear, hard to see
astonishing: very surprising

Exercise 3 Understanding the text

Write *T* for true or *F* for false for each statement.

_____ 1. Galileo published his discoveries in a newspaper.

_____ 2. People did not care much about his discoveries.

_____ 3. Galileo's telescope made it possible to see that the moon's surface was not smooth.

_____ 4. Galileo used his telescope to look at only one part of the sky.

_____ 5. With the telescope, Galileo could see Jupiter's three moons.

Exercise 4 Responding to the text

Answer the following questions about the reading.

1. What do you think scholars in 1610 said about Galileo's *Starry Messenger?*

 ____

 ____

2. Do you think people accepted Galileo's discoveries immediately? Why or why not?

 ____

 ____

3. How do you think Galileo felt when he made his discoveries with the telescope? Have you ever discovered something new or a new idea? How did you feel?

 ____

 ____

4. Galileo made many discoveries in math and physics. What are some ways we use math and/or physics in our everyday lives?

 ____

 ____

Exercise 5 Freewriting

Write for ten minutes in your journal. Choose from topics below or an idea of your own. Express your thoughts and feelings. Don't worry about mistakes.

- Galileo's discoveries changed the way people thought and saw the world. Describe an important discovery of your lifetime. How has it changed the world?
- Describe another important person in history. What did the person do? Why was it important?
- What makes people famous? Is fame always a good thing?
- Describe a person you admire. Why do you admire the person?

In **Writing Process Step 2** you will . . .

- learn about example organization.
- brainstorm ideas and specific vocabulary to use in your writing.
- determine the audience and purpose for your example paragraph.
- create an outline for your paragraph.

WRITING TASK In this unit, you will write an example paragraph that describes someone famous or someone with a special talent. You will use specific examples to explain what made the person famous, why the talents are important, and/or how the person inspires you. Go to the Web to use the Online Writing Tutor.

Exercise 1 Brainstorming ideas

Review your journal writing. Name a famous or talented person in the top box. Then think about specific examples of his or her talents. Write one example in each of the example boxes.

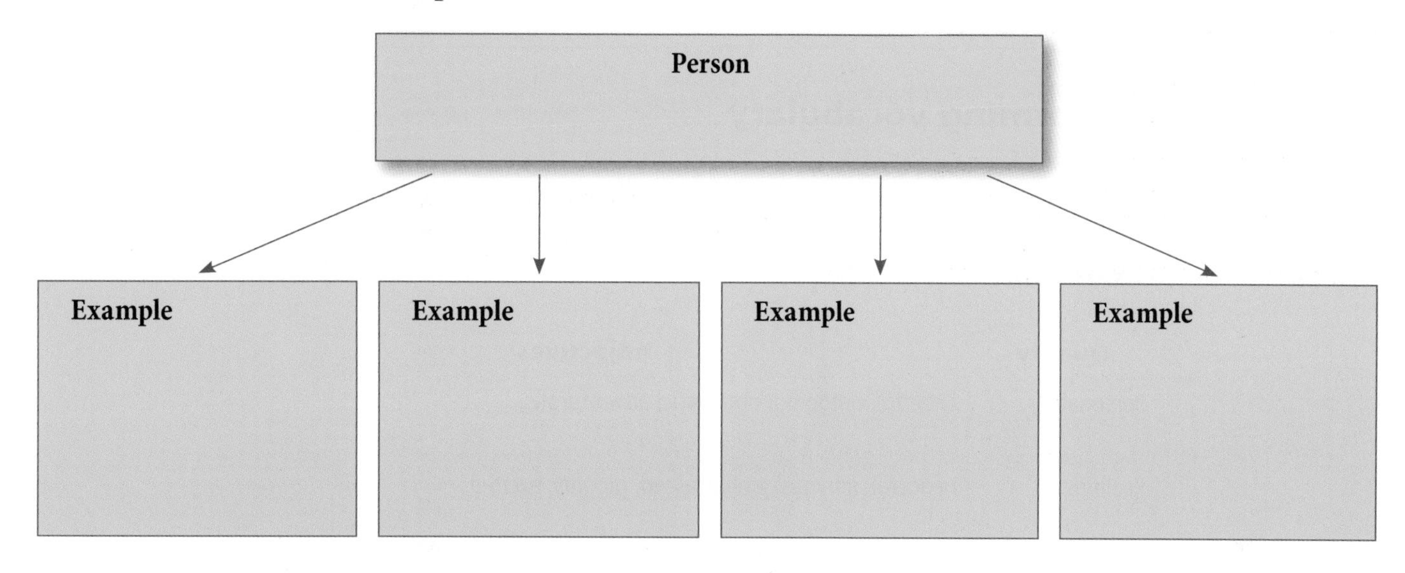

Exercise 2 Identifying audience and purpose

A. Think about your audience (the people who will read your paragraph). Write notes about this audience and what message you want to give them.

AUDIENCE	PURPOSE (MESSAGE)

B. Answer the following questions about your audience and purpose.

1. What do your readers already know about your topic?

____

____

2. What will you need to explain to help them understand your writing?

____

____

3. What do you want your readers to learn from your paragraph?

____

____

Exercise 3 Brainstorming vocabulary

A. Look at the chart below. Think about the different qualities of the person you are writing about. Add at least two new adjectives of each quality. Use your dictionary for help.

Quality	Adjectives
Personality	cheerful, outgoing, optimistic, adventurous,
Feelings	peaceful, nervous, embarrassed, gloomy, excited,
Appearance	stocky, petite, graceful, handsome,
Characteristics	intelligent, creative, courageous, organized, athletic,

B. Choose four words from the chart that you might use in your paragraph. Write a practice sentence with each word you choose.

1. Nelson Mandela was a courageous man.
2. ____
3. ____
4. ____
5. ____

Rhetorical Focus

Example Organization

An example paragraph gives specific examples so that the reader clearly understands the writer's ideas about a topic.

Topic Sentence

- The first sentence introduces the topic.
- The topic sentence also includes the controlling idea, or what the writer will say about the topic.

Supporting Sentences

- The middle sentences give examples that support the controlling idea.
- These examples give a clear picture of the writer's specific meaning.

Concluding Sentence

- The last sentence of the paragraph restates the topic and what the writer has said about it.

Exercise 4 Reading a student paragraph

Read the paragraph. Why does the writer call Nelson Mandela a "great man"?

A Great Man

The South African leader Nelson Mandela changed history, but he suffered a lot. Mandela was born to the son of a chief, and he was also named after the son of a king. He was the first in his family to attend school. His teacher gave him the English name Nelson, but his real name is Rolihlahla. His name means "troublemaker." In his life he made a lot of trouble, but it was trouble for people who did not do the right thing. Mandela's father died when Nelson was very young, but he stayed in school. He became a lawyer and started the first black law firm in South Africa. He fought apartheid, which kept black and white people separate. He went to prison for many years for what he believed in. Later, however, the people of South Africa elected him president, and he won a Nobel Peace Prize. He is a great and courageous man.

Exercise 5 Examining the student paragraph

A. Answer the following questions about the student paragraph.

1. What accomplishments of Mandela's does the writer explain?

 ____

 ____

2. In what ways did Mandela suffer? ______________________

 ____

3. What do you admire about Mandela? ______________________

 ____

4. Can you think of another person who has faced similar challenges?

 ____

 ____

B. Examine the organization of the paragraph. Respond to the questions and statements below.

1. Circle the topic and underline the controlling idea.
2. How many supporting sentences does the author include? ______________
3. What is the purpose of the second sentence of the paragraph?

 ____

 ____

4. How many sentences does the writer include about Mandela's accomplishments? ____
5. How many sentences does the writer include about how Mandela suffered? ________
6. Circle the concluding sentence. Does it restate the topic sentence? ______________
7. What is the author's opinion of Mandela? How can you tell?

 ____

 ____

Exercise 6 Writing an outline

GO ONLINE

Review your brainstorming ideas and the information on organizing an example paragraph. Then go to the Web to print out an outline template for your paragraph.

In Writing Process Step 3 you will . . .

- learn more about using examples as supporting details.
- write a first draft of your example paragraph.

Exercise 1 Reading a student paragraph

Read the paragraph. What is the game the writer refers to in the title?

My Brother's Game

My brother is an athletic guy. He likes to watch sports on television, but he loves playing sports even more. His favorite sport is soccer because it requires team work. He enjoys working with other players. He is in two leagues. One of the leagues is just for fun, so he can mess around with our cousins and friends. The other league is more serious. He has to keep himself in good condition. There are regular practices, and they work on special plays. Basketball is another of his sports. He likes basketball even though he is not so skillful. He and his friends joke while they play and have a good time. He also likes swimming, but he does not swim in competitions. Mainly he swims to stay in shape for soccer. Playing sports is the thing that he enjoys most, and he especially likes soccer because he feels happy when he and his team play well together.

Exercise 2 Examining the student paragraph

A. Answer the following questions about the paragraph.

1. What is the brother's favorite sport? What do you learn about him as a player?

 ____

 ____

2. What other sports does he participate in? ______________________________

 ____

3. What examples does the writer give to show the differences between the two soccer leagues? ______________________________

 ____

B. Examine the organization of the paragraph. Respond to the questions and statements below. Compare your answers with a partner.

1. Circle the topic and underline the controlling idea in the topic sentence.
2. Read the second sentence. What do you expect the supporting details to describe?

____

____

3. Cross out any details that do not support the topic sentence. ______________
4. Underline the concluding sentence. Does it restate the topic? ______________
5. What does the writer add to the concluding sentence that is not in the topic sentence?

____

____

Rhetorical Focus

Using Examples as Supporting Details

Effective examples are specific, and they relate clearly to the paragraph's controlling idea. Effective examples provide new information. They do not simply restate the topic sentence.

Read the following topic sentence.

topic	controlling idea
My mother	is a good neighbor.

Now read the following supporting sentences. They support the controlling idea by giving concrete, specific examples.

She always invites people from our neighborhood over for dinner.

Every year she hosts a back-to-school party for the children on our block.

Now read these sentences, which are not effective examples.

She enjoys gardening. *(not clearly related to the controlling idea)*

She is a wonderful person to live by. *(restates the controlling idea)*

An example often begins with the phrase *For example*, or *For instance*, followed by a comma.

He likes to stay in shape. **For example,** he runs six miles every day before work.

Sometimes writers use a semicolon to connect a general sentence with a specific example beginning with *for example* or *for instance.*

Our teacher is entertaining**; for instance**, sometimes he uses comic strips to teach grammar.

Exercise 3 Identifying specific examples

Read the following topic sentences. Then put a check (✓) next to the examples that support the topic sentence in more specific ways. You may add more than one check per item.

1. To become a good writer, a student should write often.

    _____ a. For example, she should try to write every day because writing is important.

    __✓__ b. For example, she should keep a journal and write in it every evening before bed.

    _____ c. For example, she can use a computer.

2. Living in the city is challenging in many ways.

    _____ a. City dwellers usually pay a lot of money to live in a small apartment.

    _____ b. It is difficult to live in a city because of the lifestyle in cities.

    _____ c. People who live in the city have to breathe polluted air.

3. My sister is easy to tease.

    _____ a. For instance, many people like to joke with her.

    _____ b. For instance, I often tell her that I am getting married, and she always believes me.

    _____ c. For instance, she has a cheerful personality, and she does not get angry when I make jokes about her hair styles.

4. This school offers a lot of opportunities to students.

    _____ a. There are many clubs and organizations for students to join.

    _____ b. The school tries to help students.

    _____ c. The school has a career counseling center that offers advice and workshops for students.

5. The world is becoming a more connected place.

    _____ a. For instance, it is easy to see that many things are changing in the world.

    _____ b. For instance, new forms of communication make it easy for people from different countries to work together on projects.

    _____ c. For instance, international travel for business has increased over the years.

Exercise 4 Making examples specific

Read the sentences below. Underline the example. Then revise each example to make it more specific.

1. I have a very patient cat. For instance, she never gives up.

   For instance, she can sit in front of a mouse hole for hours.

2. My doctor is a caring person. For example, he is very nice to patients.

3. The neighbors in my apartment building are noisy. For example, I can't sleep at night because they make a lot of noise.

4. My friend has a great sense of humor. For example, she always makes me laugh.

5. My nephew is naughty. For instance, he is always getting into trouble.

6. My friend is very athletic. For example, she can play many sports.

7. My mother is a talented potter. For instance, she makes pottery.

8. The center is a green building. For example, it uses green energy.

Exercise 5 Writing specific examples

Write two examples as supporting details for each of the following topic sentences. Make sure the examples are specific.

1. My friend loves animals.
   She always brings homeless animals to the pet shelter.
   She takes care of several animals in her home.
2. I am a busy person.
   ____
   ____
3. There are many things to see in my city.
   ____
   ____
4. Cell phones are useful for many different situations.
   ____
   ____
5. My country is beautiful.
   ____
   ____
6. My neighbors are generous.
   ____
   ____
7. Hybrid cars are economical.
   ____
   ____
8. Some of my favorite foods are very healthy.
   ____
   ____

Exercise 6 Writing a first draft

GO ONLINE

Review your outline. Then write the first draft of your example paragraph about someone famous or someone with a special talent. Go to the Web to use the Online Writing Tutor.

Exercise 7 Peer editing a first draft

A. After writing a first draft, it is helpful to get feedback on your ideas. Exchange paragraphs with two other people. For each paragraph you read, answer the Peer Editor's Questions on a separate piece of paper. Then discuss your responses.

GO ONLINE

Peer Editor's Questions

1. What is your favorite part of the paragraph?
2. What is the topic of this paragraph?
3. Is the subject famous? If so, why?
4. What talents does the subject have?
5. What questions do you have about the subject?
6. What parts of the paragraph need more examples?

Go to the Web to print out a peer editor's worksheet.

B. Review your feedback and the organization guidelines on page 59. Make notes for your revision. In this step, you may add, remove, or rewrite information to clarify your ideas.

In Writing Process Step 4 you will . . .

- learn about the simple present.
- learn about subject-verb agreement.
- edit your first draft and write a final draft.

Now that you have written a first draft, it is time to edit. When you edit, you make changes that will improve your writing and correct mistakes.

Language and Grammar Focus

GO ONLINE

The Simple Present

Use the simple present to express habits and routines.

I wake up at 6:00 every day.

Also use the simple present to write about general truths and scientific facts.

Babies are a great responsibility. Earth revolves around the sun.

Forming the Simple Present

Follow these rules to form the simple present.

When the subject is first person *I, we*, second person *you*, or third person plural *they*, use the base form of the verb.

We **exercise** every day.

When the subject of a sentence is a third person singular pronoun *he, she, it*, a singular name *Ken, Damascus*, or a singular noun *my friend, the boy*, add *–s* or *–es* to the base form of the verb.

He **works** in Buenos Aires.

To form negative statements, use *do/does* + *not* + the base form of the verb.

Ming **does not go** to school.

> Contractions such as *don't* and *doesn't* are not appropriate for written academic English.

AFFIRMATIVE STATEMENTS		
SUBJECT	**BASE FORM OF VERB OR BASE FORM OF VERB + -*S*/-*ES***	
I You	**eat**	
He She It	**eats**	fish.
We They	**eat**	

NEGATIVE STATEMENTS			
SUBJECT	***DO/DOES* + *NOT***	**BASE FORM OF VERB**	
I You	**do not**		
He She It	**does not**	**eat**	fish.
We They	**do not**		

Exercise 1 Practicing with the simple present

Complete these sentences with information about people. Use a verb in the simple present other than the verb *be*.

1. My father reads a book every week.
2. My cousin ______________________________
3. Most of my classmates ______________________________
____
4. My best friend ______________________________
5. The children in my neighborhood ______________________________
____
6. My teacher ______________________________
7. My favorite actor ______________________________
8. My parents ______________________________

Language and Grammar Focus

Subject-Verb Agreement

A verb must agree in number with its subject. Consider the examples. In the first sentence, a plural verb form *are* follows a plural pronoun *we*. However, in the second sentence, a singular form *is* follows the plural subject *we*. This sentence is incorrect.

> We **are** tired.
>
> x We is tired. (INCORRECT)

Use a plural verb following two or more nouns that are joined by *and*.

> Sachiko and her sister **live** in Kyoto.

Use a singular verb following a group noun when it talks about the group as a whole.

> The class **goes** on a field trip every month.

Use a singular verb following a noun in expressions that refer to a single member of a group.

> One of the students **owns** a restaurant.
>
> The leader of the wolves always **eats** first.

Exercise 2 Practicing subject-verb agreement

Complete each sentence with the correct form of a verb from the box.

cook / cooks	practice / practices	receive / receives
own / owns	do not work / does not work	take / takes

1. The team ___practices___ at the stadium each morning.
2. One of my brothers ____________ a brand new car.
3. Dina and Hala ____________ breakfast and dinner every day.
4. My sister and her friend ____________ on weekends.
5. Her fan club ____________ at least 100 letters a week.
6. Susan ____________ the train when she travels.

Exercise 3 Editing a paragraph

Read and edit the paragraph. There are nine more mistakes in subject-verb agreement.

My Talented Sisters

My sisters are both talented people. Vanessa and Rita ~~is~~ are musicians. Vanessa is a piano player, and Rita play the guitar. They are students at the High School for the Performing Arts. Vanessa and some other girls in her class is guest performers at community events nearly every weekend. This are good practice for them because they wants to play professionally one day. My other sister, Rita, is younger than Vanessa. She is not ready to perform yet, but she play the guitar very well. She usually perform for our family. My sisters works hard. Every day when they comes home, they play music for us. We feels lucky to have such talented people in our family.

Exercise 4 Editing your first draft and rewriting

Review your paragraph for mistakes. Use the checklist below. Then write a final draft. Go to the Web to use the Online Writing Tutor.

GO ONLINE

Editor's Checklist

Put a check (✓) as appropriate.

CONTENT AND ORGANIZATION

○ 1. Does your topic sentence introduce the person you are writing about?

○ 2. Does your paragraph include supporting sentences to explain your main idea?

○ 3. Does your paragraph include examples of the person's accomplishments?

○ 4. Do you include a concluding sentence that restates your main idea?

LANGUAGE

○ 5. Did you check for subject-verb agreement?

○ 6. Did you use verbs in the simple present correctly?

○ 7. Did you check to make sure there are no contractions?

○ 8. Did you capitalize the first letter of each sentence and use end punctuation?

Go to the Web to print out a peer editor's worksheet.

In **Review** you will . . .

- practice using specific examples in writing.
- practice using the simple present and subject-verb agreement in writing.

In Putting It All Together, you will review what you learned in this unit.

Exercise 1 Identifying examples as supporting details

Read the topic sentences and the examples that follow. Then put a check (✓) next to the examples that support the topic sentence.

1. Computers have made students' lives easier.

_____ a. They can ask questions of their instructors by email.

_____ b. They can edit their papers easily by deleting their errors and typing new words or sentences.

_____ c. They can form study groups and discuss topics in the library.

_____ d. They can research information on the Internet.

2. Nabila is someone who is always ready to help.

_____ a. For example, she enjoys buying herself clothes.

_____ b. For example, she is willing to lend her friends money if they ask for it.

_____ c. For example, she takes time off to take care of a sick grandmother.

_____ d. For example, she always asks if there is anything she can do for her friends.

3. Shopping online is more convenient than shopping at a department store.

_____ a. You can shop online at any time of the day.

_____ b. You can compare prices at several stores when shopping online.

_____ c. You cannot touch the fabric of the clothes you order.

_____ d. Since you do not have to leave your house, you will save on gas and time.

4. Reading is an important way to practice a new language.

_____ a. For instance, reading improves vocabulary.

_____ b. For instance, it is difficult to learn a new language.

_____ c. For instance, reading helps people learn sentence patterns.

_____ d. For instance, reading allows you to practice a new language.

5. The birth of my son helped me to become more patient.

_____ a. I exercised more to stay healthy for my son.

_____ b. I had to sit still for hours holding him in my arms until he fell sleep.

_____ c. Sometimes I had to spend up to two hours trying to feed him.

_____ d. When he was older, I went to movies with him.

Exercise 2 Writing specific examples

Write two examples as supporting details for each of the following topic sentences.

1. College students have a stressful life.

 ____

 ____

2. There are many advantages to being organized.

 ____

 ____

3. Most people have good memories of high school.

 ____

 ____

4. My experiences with computers have been positive.

 ____

 ____

5. Taking a vacation on the beach is a lot of fun.

 ____

 ____

Exercise 3 Using the simple present

Complete the following sentences with information that includes a verb in the simple present.

1. Writing a good paragraph ______________________________
2. Careful drivers ______________________________
3. A tourist ______________________________
4. My hometown ______________________________
5. A hero ______________________________
6. A smart phone ______________________________

Exercise 4 Practicing subject-verb agreement

Complete each sentence with the correct form of a verb from the box.

watches / watch	does not agree / do not agree	performs / perform
drives / drive	shares / share	studies / study

1. Marcos and I ______________________________ to work together twice a week.
2. My favorite band ______________________________ at the state fair every year.
3. The president of the organization ______________________________ with the committee's recommendation.
4. One of my sisters ______________________________ too much television.
5. Korea and China ______________________________ a border.
6. He ______________________________ English and economics at the university.

Exercise 5 Editing a paragraph

Read and edit the paragraph. There are eight mistakes in subject-verb agreement.

Trust

The most important quality of a friend is honesty. An honest friend never lie about anything. She tell you, for example, if she disagree with you on an issue. When you ask for advice, she tells you the truth even when it is difficult. When you asks an honest opinion about the clothes you are wearing, she tells you if they are inappropriate. If you does something bad, an honest friend do not hesitate to give you sincere feedback. This honesty result in trust between you and your friend. In short, honesty are the most important characteristic that I look for in a friend.

In Timed Writing you will . . .

- practice writing with a time limit.

Practice your test-taking skills with the following practice topic. Read the prompt. Then follow the steps below.

> **Write an example paragraph about an ideal English teacher. Provide examples of the teacher's most important characteristics.**

Step 1 BRAINSTORMING: 5 minutes

What characteristics must a good English teacher have? Write down as many of these characteristics as you can on a separate piece of paper. Then choose one characteristic that is the most important to you. Write four specific examples for that characteristic.

Step 2 OUTLINING: 5 minutes

Fill in the chart with ideas for your writing.

Topic Sentence	
Topic and Controlling Idea Introduce the topic and what you will say about it.	
Supporting Sentences	
Example 1 Provide an example that supports your main idea about the topic.	
Example 2 Use specific examples.	
Concluding Sentence	
Restatement of Topic Sentence Restate your topic and explain why the characteristics are important.	

Step 3 WRITING: 25 minutes

Use your brainstorming notes and outline to write your paragraph on a separate piece of paper.

Step 4 EDITING: 10 minutes

When you have finished your paragraph, check it for mistakes. Use the checklist below.

Editor's Checklist

Put a check (✓) as appropriate.

○ 1. Does the topic sentence introduce the topic and contain a controlling idea?

○ 2. Does the paragraph include specific examples to help the reader understand your ideas?

○ 3. Do the examples support the topic and controlling idea?

○ 4. Does the paragraph have a concluding sentence that restates the topic sentence?

○ 5. Did you use the simple present correctly?

○ 6. Do all the subjects and verbs agree?

○ 7. Did you capitalize the first letter of each sentence and use end punctuation?

Go to the Web to print out a peer editor's worksheet.

Test-Taking Tip

To make sure your ideas are all connected, read your paragraph again sentence by sentence. Repeat the topic sentence before each supporting sentence to be sure that each sentence relates to the topic sentence.

Topics for Future Writing

Write an example paragraph on one of the following topics.

Health: More and more, people are concerned about staying healthy. Why is it important to stay healthy? What are some examples of ways people can live more healthy lifestyles?

Hospitality: Write a paragraph about a successful hotel or restaurant you have visited. Why is it successful? Discuss the location, staff, service, or other examples that illustrate your point.

Mathematics: Often when students learn math in school, they don't realize how much they will use it later in their lives. Why is math important? What are some of the ways people use math in their everyday lives?

Medicine: Write a paragraph about good health-care providers. What qualities should these people have? What should they do? How should they act?

Political Science: What are the qualities of a good leader? Give examples of some strong leaders and why you believe they are or were successful.

UNIT 4

Process Paragraphs

Academic Focus Journalism

Unit Goals

Rhetorical Focus

- process organization

Language and Grammar Focus

- time-order words in process paragraphs
- imperatives
- modals of advice, necessity, and prohibition

A process paragraph explains how to do something step by step. If the process paragraph is written clearly, the reader should be able to follow the steps to complete the task.

Exercise 1 Thinking about the topic

Discuss the picture with a partner.

- What do you see in the picture?
- What is the person doing?
- What do you think the person should do if the shark attacks him?
- Have you ever been frightened by another creature? Explain why and what happened.

Exercise 2 Reading about the topic

Journalists investigate and report information for newspapers or magazines. This article is about shark attacks. What should you do if a shark attacks you?

How to Fight off a Shark

Although sharks seldom attack humans, it is a good idea to be prepared when you swim in the ocean. First, avoid **sandbars** because these are areas where sharks find their **prey**. You will not want them to think that you are competition for food or that you are a source of food. Second, swim in groups. Sharks seldom attack groups of people. Also, avoid swimming at night. You will not see sharks as easily in the dark, and sharks often attack at this time of day. If you do see a shark, leave the water as quickly as possible. Do not approach the shark or get in its way. If a shark is coming toward you, make yourself look large or **menacing** so that the shark will not think that you are easy to attack. Finally, if a shark attacks you, fight back. Hit the shark's eyes or **gills**. These areas are most sensitive to pain. Make quick, sharp **jabs** to these areas. Let the shark know that you are not **defenseless**. Keep up the fight as you make your way to shore. Once you are on land, bandage any injuries, and do not go back in the water. Report the shark attack to lifeguards or the police so that other swimmers do not get hurt.

sandbars: underwater hills
prey: a person or animal that is hunted by another animal
menacing: threatening or scary
gills: slits located in the sides of sharks that allow them to breathe
jabs: fast blows, usually done with the fist
defenseless: unable to protect oneself

Exercise 3 Understanding the text

Write *T* for true or *F* for false for each statement.

_____ 1. Sharks come close to sandbars when they are hungry.

_____ 2. It is impossible to survive a shark attack.

_____ 3. Most sharks will not attack humans.

_____ 4. If a shark attacks you, you should hit it in the nose.

_____ 5. If a shark attacks you, you should not fight back.

_____ 6. Sharks are more likely to attack if you look defenseless.

Exercise 4 Responding to the text

Answer the following questions about the reading.

1. Why do sharks attack humans?

____

____

2. What do you think government officials should do to protect sharks and humans?

____

____

3. What would you do if you saw a shark?

____

____

Exercise 5 Freewriting

Write for ten minutes in your journal. Choose from topics below or an idea of your own. Express your thoughts and feelings. Don't worry about mistakes.

- The writer described how to fight off a shark when it attacks. Explain what to do when an animal (or person) frightens or attacks you.
- What steps can a person take to have a good travel experience?
- What are you good at? (for example, repairing something or cooking) Explain how to do it.
- Describe how to prepare for a test.

In **Writing Process Step 2** you will . . .

- learn about process organization.
- brainstorm ideas and specific vocabulary to use in your writing.
- determine the audience and purpose for your process paragraph.
- create an outline for your paragraph.

WRITING TASK In this unit, you will write a process paragraph about something you know how to do. What are the steps for doing this task? How will knowing this skill help your readers? Go to the Web to use the Online Writing Tutor.

Exercise 1 Brainstorming ideas

A. To prepare for writing "Royalty in Your Garden," the student writer filled in this chart. Read the student paragraph. Then complete the chart.

Topic Sentence: Roses are easy to grow if you follow these steps.

Steps	Main Step	Supporting Details
1	Buy rose plants, potting soil, and rose food.	Choose only two or three rose bushes to start.
2	Look for a sunny place in your garden.	Roses love sunshine.
3		Use a shovel to dig the hole and add a little potting soil and rose food.
4	Transplant your roses from the pot to the hole.	Cover the roots with more potting soil.
5	Finally, give your new roses a big drink of water.	
6		When winter comes, your roses will lose their flowers and leaves and look dead. As a result, you might think about discarding them. Do not do that. Instead, cut off the thin stems with garden shears so that the bush becomes stronger the next spring.

B. **Fill in the chart below with information for your own paragraph.**

Steps	Main Step	Supporting Details
1		
2		
3		
4		
5		

Exercise 2 Identifying audience and purpose

A. **Examine the audience and purpose of the student paragraph about growing roses. Answer the following questions.**

1. Who would most likely read this text?
   a. someone who is just learning to garden
   b. someone who grows roses often
   c. a professional gardener

2. Where would you most likely find the paragraph? (Choose all that apply.)
   a. a gardening website
   b. a gardening book
   c. a magazine
   d. a professional journal for gardeners
   e. a college textbook in agriculture

3. What is the purpose of the paragraph?
   a. to encourage readers to plant roses
   b. to teach readers how to plant roses
   c. to show the advantages of planting roses

B. **On a separate piece of paper, write about the audience and purpose of your paragraph.**

Exercise 3 Brainstorming vocabulary

A. Add three words or expressions to each list. Then circle any words that you might use in your process paragraph.

Verbs	Nouns
Measure	the distance, the length,
Use	a knife, a hammer,
Complete	a form, a chart,
Check	the website, the prices,
Insert	a screw, a wire,
Ask	for advice, a counselor,

B. On a separate piece of paper, define and explain the unfamiliar words that you plan to use in your own paragraph.

Rhetorical Focus

Process Organization

A process paragraph describes the steps necessary to perform a process or task.

Topic Sentence

- The topic sentence introduces the process that the writer will explain.

Supporting Sentences

- The middle sentences describe a sequence of steps.
- The supporting sentences give detailed information about each step in the process.
- These sentences may also give background details to help define the process for the reader.
- Supporting sentences may also include the tools needed for the task.

Concluding Sentence

- The paragraph ends with a concluding sentence that restates the topic sentence using different words.
- This sentence may explain why the process is useful or necessary.
- The concluding sentence may also include a suggestion, prediction, or warning to help the reader do the task more easily.

Exercise 4 Reading a student paragraph

Read the paragraph. What does the word *royalty* in the title refer to?

Royalty in Your Garden

Roses are royalty among flowers. Many people say they are as difficult to maintain as kings and queens, but roses are actually quite easy to grow if you follow these steps. First, go to a nursery to purchase the rose plants, potting soil, and rose food. Choose only two or three rose bushes to start. Later, after you feel more confident about planting roses, you can plant more. After you bring your rose plants home, look for a sunny spot in your garden because roses love sunshine. Then dig a deep hole with a shovel, and add some potting soil and rose food. Next, take the roses out of the pot. Be careful to prevent the stems from breaking. Then transplant your roses from the pot to the hole. Cover the roots with more potting soil. Finally, give your new roses a big drink of water. As long as they have sunshine and water, your roses will stay healthy all summer. When winter comes, your roses will lose their flowers and leaves. They will look dead. As a result, you might think about discarding them. Do not do that. Instead, this is the best time to prune your roses. Cut off the thin stems with garden shears so that the bush can become stronger the next spring. If you continue to take care of your roses in this simple way, they will produce beautiful flowers year after year.

Exercise 5 Examining the student paragraph

A. Answer the following questions about the student paragraph.

1. What is the purpose of the first sentence? ______________________________

____

2. Which sentence is the topic sentence? ______________________________

____

3. Are there any missing steps or explanations? Explain. ______________________

____

4. Would you be able to plant a rose bush after reading this paragraph? ________

B. Examine the organization of the paragraph. Respond to the questions and statements below. Compare answers with a partner.

1. Which of the following statements best describes the main idea of the paragraph? (Check one.)

 _____ a. Roses are very special flowers.

 _____ b. Growing roses is easy.

 _____ c. Roses are difficult to grow.

2. Which of the following types of details does the writer include in the paragraph? (Check all that apply.)

 _____ a. the tools that are necessary for growing roses

 _____ b. warnings about what not to do when growing roses

 _____ c. steps that gardeners should take when growing roses

 _____ d. the result of the task

3. Circle the words in the paragraph that signal each step.

4. Underline the concluding sentence twice. Which statement below best describes the concluding sentence? (Check one.)

 _____ a. It is a warning about what can go wrong.

 _____ b. It tells the expected result of the process.

 _____ c. It is a summary of the main steps.

Exercise 6 Writing an outline

GO ONLINE

Review your brainstorming ideas and the information on organizing process paragraphs. Then go to the Web to print out an outline template for your paragraph.

In **Writing Process Step 3** you will . . .

- learn to use time-order words in a process paragraph.
- write a first draft of your process paragraph.

Exercise 1 Reading a student paragraph

Read the paragraph. What is the secret to a successful vacation?

The Secret to a Successful Vacation

Imagine that you are on vacation at the beach. You open your suitcase to discover that you have forgotten your swimsuit! This and other disasters can be avoided if you follow certain steps when you pack your suitcase. The first step is to review your travel plans. Make a list, and save it so that you can check your items before you leave. Next, gather the items you will need for your activities. For example, if you plan to go hiking in the mountains, you will need hiking boots and comfortable clothes. Try to mix and match fewer pieces of clothing and shoes by choosing a color or colors that match. Now that you have your travel plans and list, you are ready to pack. Start with large items such as books or shoes. Stuff socks into your shoes to save space. Then place shoes in plastic bags and fit them into the corners of your suitcase. There should be plenty of room for the clothes. To avoid wrinkles, layer your clothes and roll them up. Put the rolls of clothing into the suitcase. Then put in the smaller items. Finally, before you close your suitcase, check your list. Make sure you have not forgotten your swimsuit! Take your time when you pack your suitcase because a well-packed suitcase is the secret to a good travel experience.

Exercise 2 Examining the student paragraph

A. Answer the following questions about the student paragraph.

1. How is this process similar to or different from the way you pack a suitcase?

____

____

2. Why is it important to review travel plans before packing a suitcase?

____

____

3. Who is the audience for this text? ______________________________

____

4. What other steps would you add to this process? ______________________

____

B. Examine the organization of the paragraph. Then complete the chart below. Compare your answers with a partner.

Topic Sentence: ______________________________________

____

Steps	Main Step	Supporting Details
1	Review your travel plans	Make a list of your travel destinations and activities and save it so that you can check your items before you leave.
2		
3		
4		

Concluding Sentence: ______________________________________

____

Language and Grammar Focus

Using Time-Order Words in Process Paragraphs

Time-order words tell the order of steps in a process. You can use *first* and *second* to indicate the first two steps in a process. Use *next, then, later,* or *after that* to add more steps. The word *finally* marks the last step in the process.

First, make a list.

Second, select your clothes.

Next, place your shoes in the corners.

Then arrange your clothes in neat layers.

Later, add last-minute items such as medications.

After that, roll up the clothes to avoid wrinkles.

Finally, check your list for any forgotten items.

> *Then* is not followed by a comma.
> Connectors link two clauses together. Connectors like *before* and *after* can also function as time-order words when they link two steps in a process.
>
> **Before** you close your suitcase, check your list.
>
> Begin packing **after** you have eliminated all unnecessary items.

Exercise 3 Using time-order words to identify the sequence of steps

Number the steps in the following process according to how they should be followed. Use the time-order words to help you decide the correct order.

It is easy to have a good dinner celebration if you follow some easy steps.

_____ a. Next, make a list of people whom you would like to invite.

_____ b. After your house is clean, go shopping for food, flowers, and decorations.

_____ c. Then make a funny or pretty invitation and email it to your friends.

_____ d. Finally, turn on the music, and wait for the guests to arrive.

_____ e. Before the guests arrive, decorate the house, set the table, and take a shower.

_____ f. After you have everything you need, plan a meal. Make sure you can cook most of it before your guests arrive.

_____ g. A few days before the dinner, start cleaning your house.

__1__ h. First, choose an appropriate date at least two weeks before the dinner.

Exercise 4 Practicing with time-order words

Read the following paragraph. Fill in the blanks with appropriate time-order words. Remember to use proper punctuation.

One big challenge that many people like is running in a marathon. A marathon is a race for runners. It is more than twenty-six miles long. It is very hard to complete the race. If you want to run the entire course, you have to train for a long time. ____First,____ (1.) buy a good pair of comfortable running shoes. Then begin your running practice. You will need to train for at least six months ____________ (2.) you run in the race. At first, try to run three to six miles at least four times a week. You must also stretch before and after a run to avoid tight muscles. ____________ (3.) your body is accustomed to longer runs, you can work on your strength by doing sprints, or short, fast runs. ____________ (4.) lengthen your runs to ten or twelve miles. Make sure you drink plenty of water. Water is important for your muscles. Water will also help you avoid dehydration. When the day of the race is close, check your shoes. You might need a new pair. Wear the new shoes during your training so you can break them in before the race. The night before you race, eat a lot of carbohydrates such as pasta or bread. These carbohydrates will give you energy for the big day. ____________ (5.) on the day of the race, get up early and drink plenty of water. After all this hard work, you should feel confident, strong, and ready to go.

Exercise 5 Writing the steps in a process

Read the following topics. With a partner, write some important steps for each process. Use appropriate time-order words.

Topic: how to buy a used car

Step 1: ______________________________

____

____

Step 2: ______________________________

____

____

Step 3: ______________________________

____

____

Topic: how to use a search engine

Step 1: ______________________________

____

____

Step 2: ______________________________

____

____

Step 3: ______________________________

____

____

Exercise 6 Writing a first draft

GO ONLINE

Review your outline. Then write the first draft of your process paragraph about something you know how to do that might be helpful to someone else. Go to the Web to use the Online Writing Tutor.

Exercise 7 Peer editing a first draft

A. **After writing a first draft, it is helpful to get feedback on your ideas. Exchange paragraphs with two other people. For each paragraph you read, answer the Peer Editor's Questions on a separate piece of paper. Then discuss your responses.**

GO ONLINE

Peer Editor's Questions

1. What is your favorite part of the paragraph?
2. What process is this writer describing?
3. Who do you think will be interested in reading this paragraph? Why?
4. Does the writer start the paragraph with a topic sentence?
5. Are all the steps explained clearly? How?
6. What questions do you have for the writer?

Go to the Web to print out a peer editor's worksheet.

B. **Review your feedback and the organization guidelines on page 83. Make notes for your revision. In this step, you may add, remove, or rewrite information to clarify your ideas.**

In **Writing Process Step 4** you will . . .

- learn about imperatives.
- learn to identify and use modals of advice, necessity, and prohibition.
- edit your first draft and write a final draft.

Writing Process Step 4 | Editing Your Writing

Now that you have written a first draft, it is time to edit. When you edit, you make changes that will improve your writing and correct mistakes.

Language and Grammar Focus

GO ONLINE

Using Imperatives

Use **imperative sentences** to give instructions, directions, or to give steps in a process.

The verb in an imperative addresses the reader or listener directly.

Attach the bait to the hook. (You)

The imperative uses the base form of the verb.

Hold the fishing rod gently in your right hand.

An imperative sentence does not require a subject. The subject *you* is implied.

Be quiet or you may disturb the fish.

For a negative imperative, use *do not.*

Do not let your finger get caught in the string.

Exercise 1 Identifying imperatives

Put a check (✓) next to the imperative sentences.

__✓__ 1. Buy a good quality tape.

____ 2. It is important to start early in the morning to avoid the heat.

____ 3. Get down on your hands and knees and crawl under the smoke.

____ 4. Try not to get chili powder in your eyes.

____ 5. You should ask a professional to dispose of the used motor oil.

____ 6. With your left hand, grab the red handle and pull it.

____ 7. Getting out of a traffic jam is not too difficult if you follow this procedure.

____ 8. It is useful to get the fabric wet before you dye it.

____ 9. Type in the address, and then click Search.

____ 10. It is a good idea to check your tires before you start the car.

____ 11. You must turn off the electricity before you change the bulb.

____ 12. Never shake a soda before you open it.

____ 13. Do not feed wild animals.

Exercise 2 Using imperatives

Rewrite the following sentences as imperatives.

1. It is necessary to check the horse's back for sticks and insects before you put on the saddle blanket.

   Check the horse's back for sticks and insects before you put on the saddle blanket.

2. It is a good idea to fill water bottles and put them in the freezer the night before.

   ____

3. You should dress in comfortable clothing and sneakers or sandals.

   ____

4. It is important to debug your hard drive periodically.

   ____

5. You need to replace the water in the tank every week or two.

   ____

6. You must not leave the fire unattended.

   ____

Language and Grammar Focus

GO ONLINE

Modals of Advice, Necessity, and Prohibition

Should and *must* are **modal verbs**. You can use modals to give advice, rules, or warnings. Modal verbs come before the base form of the verb.

You **should eat** more vegetables.   You **must arrive** by eight o'clock.

Advice

In a process paragraph, use the modal *should* to offer advice, tips, and suggestions for being more successful.

You **should** remove all jewelry before working with clay.

Necessity

Use the modal *must* to explain rules and laws that affect a process. The word *must* is stronger. It tells readers that something is absolutely necessary.

You **must** wear protective goggles when you use a saw.

Use *do not have to* to say that something is not necessary.

You **do not have to** pay a fee to enter the museum.

Prohibition

When you want to offer a warning or prohibit someone from doing something, use *should* and *must* with *not* and the base form of the verb.

You **should not** open the oven while the cake is baking.

You **must not** light a match while working with gas.

AFFIRMATIVE STATEMENTS WITH *SHOULD* AND *MUST*		
SUBJECT	*SHOULD/MUST*	BASE FORM OF VERB
I You He She It We They	**should** **must**	**participate.**

NEGATIVE STATEMENTS WITH *SHOULD* AND *MUST*		
SUBJECT	*SHOULD/MUST + NOT*	BASE FORM OF VERB
I You He She It We They	**should not** **must not**	**participate.**

NEGATIVE STATEMENTS WITH *HAVE TO*			
SUBJECT	*DO/DOES + NOT*	*HAVE TO*	BASE FORM OF VERB
I You	do not	**have to**	**participate.**
He She It	does not		
We They	do not		

Exercise 3 Using modals of advice, necessity, and prohibition

Complete each sentence with *should* or *must*. Explain why you chose each modal.

1. You ___should___ start early in the morning to avoid the traffic.
   This is advice, but it is not a necessity.
2. You __________ have a license to drive a car.
   ____
3. You __________ not write text messages while you drive a car.
   ____
4. You look tired. You __________ get a good night's sleep.
   ____
5. You __________ not leave a baby alone in a bathtub.
   ____

Exercise 4 Practicing with modal verbs

Use modal verbs to write one affirmative and one negative sentence about each topic.

1. babysitting
   You should ask about the child's bedtime.
   You must not leave the child alone outside.
2. changing a lightbulb
   ____
   ____
3. applying for a job
   ____
   ____
4. driving in the rain
   ____
   ____

Exercise 5 Practice using modals

Use the ideas in the box to write sentences to help new drivers follow laws and drive safely. Use *have to, should (not),* or *must (not).*

using cell phones while driving

using signals when changing lanes

smoking while pumping gas

eating while driving

stopping to let children cross the street

driving with lights on during the day

Exercise 6 Editing a paragraph

Read and edit the paragraph. There are six more mistakes in imperatives and modal verbs.

If you are serious about managing your time better, you should follow~~ing~~ this procedure. It will help you to have more control over your time. First, you need to figure out how you actually spend your time. You make a list of all the things you do daily. Writing down how much time you spend on each thing. Include activities like talking on the telephone or buying a cup of coffee. Your list will be quite long. Then find the activities that you can eliminate from your daily routine. It may be hard to give up a trip to the coffee shop, but you can do it. You must going to work, so you cannot eliminate that item, but you will probably find other items that are not necessary. You should dropped those unnecessary activities to make time for more important things. Next, prepare a schedule for yourself. Being realistic about the time of day you choose for certain activities. Make a schedule that you can follow. Not try to do too much. If you follow these steps and manage your schedule carefully, you will have a happier, more organized life.

Exercise 7 Editing your first draft and rewriting

Review your paragraph for mistakes. Use the checklist below. Then write a final draft. Go to the Web to use the Online Writing Tutor.

GO ONLINE

Editor's Checklist

Put a check (✓) as appropriate.

CONTENT AND ORGANIZATION

- ○ 1. Does your paragraph have a topic sentence?
- ○ 2. Did you include several steps that explain how to do the task?
- ○ 3. Do your supporting details (or examples) explain the steps clearly?
- ○ 4. Does your paragraph have a conclusion?

LANGUAGE

- ○ 5. Did you use imperatives to give instructions or directions?
- ○ 6. Did you use *should* to give advice and *must* to explain rules?
- ○ 7. Did you use *not* with a modal to give warnings?
- ○ 8. Did you use *do not have to* to explain that something is not necessary?

Go to the Web to print out a peer editor's worksheet.

In **Review** you will . . .

- review the use of time-order words in a process paragraph.
- practice using imperatives and modal verbs in writing.

Review | Putting It All Together

In Putting It All Together, you will review what you learned in this unit.

Exercise 1 Using time-order words

Read the following paragraph. Fill in the blanks with appropriate time-order words from the box. Use proper punctuation and capitalization.

then	second	finally	first	next

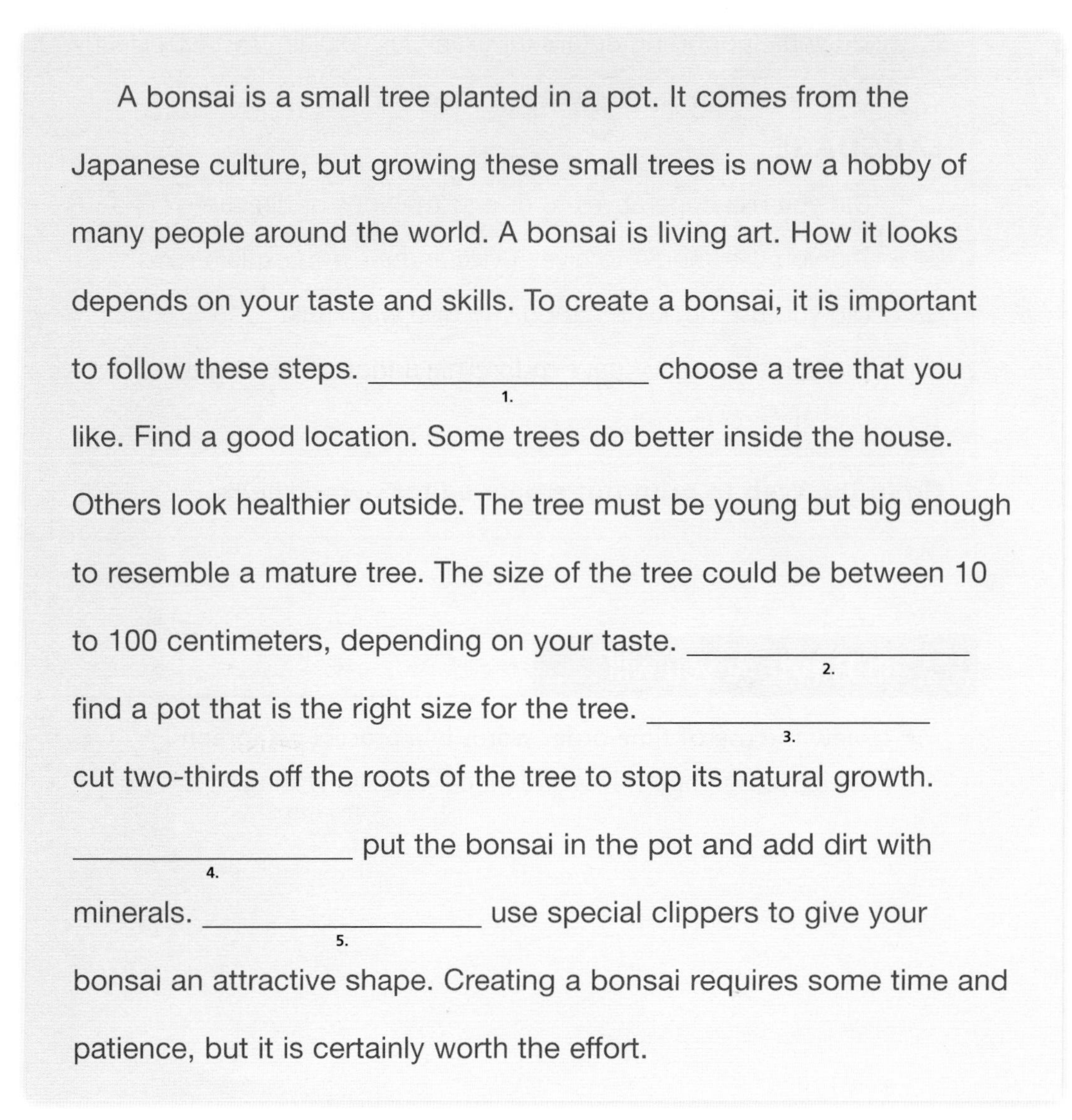

A bonsai is a small tree planted in a pot. It comes from the Japanese culture, but growing these small trees is now a hobby of many people around the world. A bonsai is living art. How it looks depends on your taste and skills. To create a bonsai, it is important to follow these steps. ____________ (1.) choose a tree that you like. Find a good location. Some trees do better inside the house. Others look healthier outside. The tree must be young but big enough to resemble a mature tree. The size of the tree could be between 10 to 100 centimeters, depending on your taste. ____________ (2.) find a pot that is the right size for the tree. ____________ (3.) cut two-thirds off the roots of the tree to stop its natural growth. ____________ (4.) put the bonsai in the pot and add dirt with minerals. ____________ (5.) use special clippers to give your bonsai an attractive shape. Creating a bonsai requires some time and patience, but it is certainly worth the effort.

Exercise 2 Using imperatives

Rewrite the following sentences as imperatives.

1. You must buy a good fishing rod.

 ____

2. You should warn the patient before you give him an injection.

 ____

3. You need to type your log-in ID and your password.

 ____

4. You need to jog slowly at first.

 ____

Exercise 3 Using *should* and *must*

Complete each sentence with *should (not)* or *must (not)*. Then explain to a partner why you chose each modal.

1. You ____________________ begin eating until the hostess does. It is not polite.
2. You ____________________ arrive on time, or the boat will leave without you.
3. We ____________________ wait until the last minute to pack.
4. You ____________________ drink plenty of water when you exercise.
5. In some countries, you ____________________ be 18 years old to drive.
6. You ____________________ leave early to get good seats.
7. She ____________________ add more salt to the soup.
8. He ____________________ drink coffee before bed.

In Timed Writing you will . . .

- practice writing with a time limit.

Practice your test-taking skills with the following practice topic.
Read the prompt. Then follow the steps below.

> Write a process paragraph. Describe steps for choosing an important gift such as a wedding gift. How do you decide what to buy? Where do you go to buy it?

Step 1 BRAINSTORMING: 5 minutes

Think about someone for whom you have bought a special gift. Write down the gift that you chose and how you decided to buy it. Try to think of three or four steps that describe the process. Think of reason(s) why each step is important and write down the reasons.

Step 2 OUTLINING: 5 minutes

Fill in the chart with ideas for your writing.

Topic Sentence	
Topic Sentence and Controlling Idea Introduce the topic and the process.	
Supporting Sentences	
Step 1 Explain the first step with details about what tools will be needed.	
Step 2 Explain the second step. Provide any necessary background information.	
Step 3 Explain the third step in the process. Provide details to help your readers.	
Concluding Sentence	
Restatement of Topic Sentence Restate the topic sentence. Include a suggestion, prediction, or warning.	

Step 3 WRITING: 25 minutes

Use your brainstorming notes and outline to write your paragraph on a separate piece of paper.

Step 4 EDITING: 10 minutes

When you have finished your paragraph, check it for mistakes. Use the checklist below.

Editor's Checklist

Put a check (✓) as appropriate.

○ 1. Does the topic sentence tell what the task is?

○ 2. Does the topic sentence contain a controlling idea?

○ 3. Do your steps give detailed information, background details, and the tools needed for the task?

○ 4. Did you use time-order words to separate the steps?

○ 5. Did you use imperatives to give directions or instructions?

○ 6. Did you use modals to express advice, necessity, and prohibition?

○ 7. Does the concluding sentence offer a suggestion or warning to help the reader understand the importance of following the steps?

○ 8. Did you capitalize the first letter of each sentence and use end punctuation?

Go to the Web to print out a peer editor's worksheet.

Test-Taking Tip

After you finish writing down the steps and reason for the steps, read the prompt again to make sure you are answering the prompt. Again, after you finish drafting, check the draft against the prompt as well.

Topics for Future Writing

Write a process paragraph on one of the following topics.

Computer Science: Explain how to develop a Web page.

Engineering: Explain how to change a battery in a car, a camera, or another electronic device.

Marketing: Explain the steps that a typical customer goes through to choose a particular brand of appliance or electronics.

Medicine: Explain what someone should expect during a typical physical checkup at a doctor's office.

Psychology: Describe the process of overcoming a psychological issue, such as stress or homesickness.

Sociology: Describe the steps involved in finding a husband or wife in a particular culture.

UNIT 5

Narrative Paragraphs

Academic Focus Psychology

Unit Goals

Rhetorical Focus

- narrative organization
- sensory and emotional details

Language and Grammar Focus

- order of events in narrative paragraphs
- the simple past
- the past continuous

In narrative writing, the writer tells a story that sets the background for an event, describes the event, and often comments on the event. In this unit, you will write a narrative paragraph that tells the story of an event in your life.

Exercise 1 Thinking about the topic

Discuss the pictures with a partner.

- Describe the children in the photographs.
- What are they doing? How do you think they feel?
- For each photograph, describe how you imagine the children live. What do they do each day? Where and with whom do they live?
- How are these children's experiences similar or different from your own childhood experiences?
- In your opinion, what are the elements of a "good" childhood?

Exercise 2 Reading about the topic

Psychology is the study of what influences our behavior and how we feel about things. As you read, think about how this family is reacting to moving into their new home. How does it affect their behavior?

A House for Mr. Biswas

They could only unpack that evening. A rough meal was prepared in the kitchen and they ate in the **chaotic** dining room. They said little. Only Shama moved and spoke without **constraint**. The beds were **mounted** upstairs. Anand slept on the **verandah**. He could feel the floor curving below him towards the **offending** wall. He placed his hand on the wall, as if that might give him some idea of its weight. At every footstep, particularly Shama's, he could feel the floor shake. When he closed his eyes he experienced a spinning, **swaying** sensation. **Hurriedly** he opened them again to **reassure** himself that the floor had not sunk further, that the house still stood.

Adapted from Naipaul, V.S. *A House for Mr. Biswas.* New York: Vintage Books, 1989.

chaotic: in a state of disorder or confusion
constraint: restriction
mounted: put in place
verandah: porch
offending: not well liked
swaying: moving back and forth
hurriedly: quickly
reassure: do something to feel less frightened

Exercise 3 Understanding the text

Write *T* for true or *F* for false for each statement.

_____ 1. In celebration of their new home, the family ate a well-prepared meal.

_____ 2. There was much conversation about the new house.

_____ 3. Anand slept on the bottom floor of the house.

_____ 4. The floors of the home are uneven, and they shake.

_____ 5. Anand fell asleep easily in his new home.

Exercise 4 Responding to the text

Answer the following questions about the reading.

1. How does the author describe the environment in the home on the family's first night?

____

____

2. What are some reasons why members of the family might not be talking?

____

____

3. What words does the author use to describe the sensation Anand feels when he is lying down? Why might he be feeling this way?

____

____

Exercise 5 Freewriting

Write for ten minutes in your journal. Choose from topics below or an idea of your own. Express your thoughts and feelings. Don't worry about mistakes.

- The writer describes the feelings Anand and his family had when they moved to a new home. What do you think happened to the family?
- Have you ever slept in a place where you felt uncomfortable? Describe your experience. What made you feel that way?
- Describe a time when you got lost. How did you feel? How did you find your way?
- Describe a difficult situation in your life. What did you learn from the experience?

In **Writing Process Step 2** you will . . .

- learn about narrative organization.
- brainstorm ideas and specific vocabulary to use in your writing.
- determine the audience and purpose for your narrative paragraph.
- create an outline for your paragraph.

Writing Process Step 2 | Brainstorming and Outlining

WRITING TASK In this unit, you will write a narrative paragraph about a challenging situation that you faced some time in your past. Go to the Web to use the Online Writing Tutor.

Exercise 1 Brainstorming ideas

A. Think about the challenging situation you will write about. Complete the chart below with details about what happened before, during, and after the situation.

The Challenging Situation: ________________________________

	Before	During	After
Who was there?			
What happened?			
How did you feel?			
What did you hear, smell, see, or taste?			

B. Tell your story to a partner. Answer your partner's questions about your challenging situation. Then add details to the chart based on your answers.

Exercise 2 Identifying audience and purpose

A. Match each sentence or phrase from the reading with its purpose.

_____ 1. A rough meal was prepared in the kitchen, and they ate in the chaotic dining room.
_____ 2. The beds were put together upstairs.
_____ 3. At every footstep, particularly Shama's, he could feel the floor shake.
_____ 4. They said little.
_____ 5. Quickly he opened them again to be sure.

a. to show that the family was quiet
b. to demonstrate that the house was not strong
c. to describe Anand's feelings
d. to indicate where the family would sleep
e. to show that things in the house were disorganized

B. As a writer's audience changes, the way he or she writes also changes. Think about the challenging situation you will write about. Then write sentences about your experience for each of the contexts below.

A potential employer has asked you to describe a challenge you have faced and how you solved it.

____

____

____

____

____

____

____

A friend or sibling is facing a difficult time, and you wish to use your experiences to advise him or her.

____

____

____

____

____

____

____

Exercise 3 Brainstorming vocabulary

With a partner, brainstorm descriptive words. List them in the blanks. Then choose one to complete each sentence.

1. I was in a/an ______________ place.

   scary, elegant, enormous, strange, ______________

2. I felt ______________.

   nervous, important, numb, ______________, ______________

3. I ______________.

   ran, cried, fell, ______________, ______________

4. The experience ______________ me.

   thrilled, matured, motivated, ______________, ______________

5. I gained a lot of ______________ from this experience.

   confidence, knowledge, friends, ______________, ______________

Rhetorical Focus

Narrative Organization

A **narrative paragraph** tells a story. Like other kinds of paragraphs you have learned about in this book, it has a topic sentence, supporting sentences, and a concluding sentence.

Topic Sentence

- The topic sentence tells the reader what the story will be about.
- It may also tell when and where the story took place.
- The topic sentence should capture the reader's interest.

Supporting Sentences

- The supporting sentences tell what happened.
- The supporting sentences explain the sequence of events.
- They include sensory details, such as what the writer saw, heard, smelled, or tasted.
- Supporting sentences also tell about the writer's feelings during the events.

Concluding Sentence

- The concluding sentence "wraps up" the story.
- The concluding sentence may include a comment about why the experience was important or what the writer learned from the experience.

Exercise 4 Reading a student paragraph

Read the paragraph. Why was the sandwich so good?

The Best Sandwich of My Life

When I was thirteen years old, I had a great surprise. My favorite soccer team was visiting from Mexico, so I went to the Grand Hotel to get autographs from some of the players. When I got there, I waited outside for a long time because I was very nervous. Finally, I told my legs to start moving. I walked in and went up to my favorite player, Sergio Verdirame to ask for his autograph. My voice was trembling, but I controlled it. He stopped to listen to me. Then an amazing thing happened. He invited me to dinner with the team. I could not believe it! Suddenly I was sitting across the table from Sergio Verdirame! I ordered a huge sandwich with everything on it. When the food came, my hands were shaking, and I could not eat or talk. After a while, I took a deep breath and said to myself, *Hey, this happens just once in your life.* I fought off my nerves and started talking with the team and enjoying my meal. They were really great guys. We had a good time laughing and joking together. That was the most delicious sandwich I ever ate because I was eating it with my hero.

Exercise 5 Examining the student paragraph

A. Answer the following questions about the student paragraph.

1. Why did the writer go to the hotel? ______________________________

____

2. What words does the writer use to show that he was nervous?

____

____

3. What do you think the writer actually said when he spoke to Sergio Verdirame?

____

____

B. Examine the organization of the paragraph. Respond to the questions and statements below. Compare answers with a partner.

1. Underline the topic sentence. What do you learn from it?

   ____

   ____

2. Read the following events from the story. Number them in the order in which they occurred.

   _____ a. The writer ordered a sandwich.

   _____ b. The writer was very nervous, and his hands were shaking.

   _____ c. The writer asked the soccer player for his autograph.

   _____ d. Sergio Verdirame invited the writer to dinner.

   _____ e. The writer overcame his fear and enjoyed his dinner.

3. In the concluding sentence, the writer explains what made him happiest. Which sentence best describes his final comment?

   a. He ate a very good sandwich.

   b. He spent time with his favorite soccer player.

   c. He overcame his fear of speaking to his heroes.

   d. He got an autograph from his favorite player.

Exercise 6 Writing an outline

GO ONLINE

Review your brainstorming ideas and the information on organizing a narrative paragraph. Then go to the Web to print out an outline template for your paragraph.

In Writing Process Step 3 you will . . .

- learn to use sensory and emotional details in a narrative paragraph.
- learn to show the order of events in a narrative paragraph.
- write a first draft of your narrative paragraph.

Exercise 1 Reading a student paragraph

Read the paragraph. How did the writer feel just before his wild experience?

Something Wild

For my 25th birthday, my favorite uncle gave me a gift certificate to go skydiving at a special place near Miami. I was happy because I wanted to do something wild. On the day of my jump, I woke up with a crazy feeling in my stomach. I could not eat breakfast because of my nerves. After we arrived at the place, I had to sign a lot of papers because of the risk involved. I signed them quickly because I did not want to think about the danger. Before I knew it, I was on the plane with my parachute on my back. The only thing I could think was, *What am I doing?* One of the staff opened the door of the plane and told me to get ready. I put my right foot over the edge and waited for the signal . . . "three, two, one . . ." and then I was free-falling, going down at almost two hundred kilometers per hour. I was shouting, and I could feel adrenaline running through me. Nearby, there was another guy taking photos. I like to take photos too. Then the parachute opened, and the next five minutes were the most incredible moments of my life. I was floating completely free, like a bird. All my problems were gone, and I could see the curve of the earth, the ocean, and faraway clouds off the shore. It was awesome. Those wonderful moments helped me to realize that I am the kind of person who likes to take risks, and I hope I always will be.

Exercise 2 Examining the student paragraph

A. Answer the following questions about the student paragraph.

1. What does the writer mean when he says that he woke up with "a crazy feeling" in his stomach? Why did he feel this way?

   ____

   ____

2. Why do you think the writer didn't want to think about the danger of skydiving?

   ____

   ____

3. Why do some parts of the story seem to go faster than other parts of the story?

   ____

   ____

4. What does the writer mean when he says "All my problems were gone"?

   ____

   ____

B. Examine the organization of the paragraph. Respond to the questions and statements below. Compare your answers with a partner.

1. Underline the topic sentence. What background details does it include?

   ____

   ____

2. Who are the people in the story?

   ____

   ____

3. Circle the words or phrases that tell the reader how the writer felt after he jumped from the plane.
4. Cross out any sentences that do not directly relate to the topic sentence.
5. Underline the concluding sentence twice. What did the writer learn from his experience?

   ____

   ____

Rhetorical Focus

Sensory and Emotional Details

To make a narrative paragraph interesting, writers include **sensory** and **emotional** details. These details help the reader form a very clear picture of the sights, sounds, smells, tastes, and feelings that the writer experienced. If the details are strong enough, the reader almost feels like he or she is able to experience the event.

- **Sensory details** give information about how something looks, smells, tastes, feels, or sounds.

  My teeth were chattering, and my legs felt like jelly.
  The morning sun warmed my back.

- **Emotional details** help the reader understand the writer's feelings.

  Suddenly, my fear vanished, and I felt confident as I looked out at the crowd.
  The sight filled me with excitement.

Exercise 3 Identifying sensory and emotional details

Read the sentences below. Write *S* next to the sentences that have sensory details. Write *E* next to the sentences that have emotional details.

__S__ 1. The morning mist brought in the smell of the ocean.

_____ 2. We were very nervous, so we called the police.

_____ 3. I had never felt such happiness.

_____ 4. The dates were sticky and sweet, and they were delicious with the hot, bitter tea.

_____ 5. I felt a sharp pain in my ankle, and I recognized the sting of a jellyfish.

_____ 6. We could hear the roar of the waterfall long before we actually saw it.

_____ 7. She was so angry when she heard the news that she threw her book across the room.

_____ 8. The soaked hikers looked up to see two beautiful rainbows spread across the desert sky.

_____ 9. We could barely sit still as we waited to hear the name of the winner.

_____ 10. The kitchen had the wonderful smell of freshly brewed coffee.

Exercise 4 Practicing with sensory details

Use sensory details to support the following sentences.

1. Our guide had an interesting fashion sense.

   He wore the same khaki pants every day, but his shirts always had colorful patterns of flowers, surfers, or other tropical scenes.

2. We ate a wonderful meal.

   ____

   ____

3. The flower garden was delightful.

   ____

   ____

4. The alley had not been taken care of for many years, and it was in bad shape.

   ____

   ____

5. My father taught me to swim in a river behind our house.

   ____

   ____

6. My mother's kitchen was everyone's favorite room.

   ____

   ____

7. We listened to the music.

   ____

   ____

8. I molded the clay in my hands.

   ____

   ____

Exercise 5 Practicing with emotional details

Use emotional details to support the following sentences.

1. I would like to forget my first job interview.

   I was so nervous my hands were wet, and so was my shirt.

2. I met my friend on the Internet.

3. At first, I did not like the new puppy, but after a while I changed my mind.

4. I began to walk down the aisle toward my future husband.

5. I walked into the cold, dark cave.

6. The test was over, and I had earned the highest score.

7. It was the first day of school, and I didn't know where to go.

8. I broke through the ribbon and ran through the finish line.

9. I slipped and fell as I reached out to shake his hand.

Language and Grammar Focus

Order of Events in Narrative Paragraphs

Writers of narrative paragraphs use **sequence words** and **expressions** to clarify the order of events in a story.

The following sequence words are used when events happen in **chronological (time) order.** These words are often used at the beginning of sentences.

first	after that	afterwards	then	later
second	eventually	next	soon	finally

First, we unpacked the car and set up our tent. **After that**, we built a fire and cooked our food.

Our entire family squeezed into the car, and **soon** we were on our way.

Showing Simultaneous Events

Writers use the following words and expressions to show that two events occurred at the same time.

meanwhile	while	at the same time that

I made coffee. **Meanwhile**, my brother tried to distract our sister.

I was planning a wedding **at the same time that** I was preparing to move.

Exercise 6 Identifying order of events

Read the sentences. Number them in the order you think they occurred.

__1__ a. A few years ago, my two older brothers and I went hiking in the mountains.

_____ b. I found the muddy trail, and we were able to return to our camp.

_____ c. We were hiking through thick pine forests.

_____ d. We left our camp on a bright winter morning.

_____ e. I realized it is very important to be careful when hiking in the mountains.

_____ f. We stopped to eat lunch, and my oldest brother said we should turn around because we were losing the trail in the snow.

_____ g. It began to snow, and we could not see well.

_____ h. Going back down the mountain was harder because it was icy and slippery, and we could not find the way because of the snow.

Exercise 7 Using sequence words and expressions

Write the sentences from Exercise 6 in paragraph form. Use some of the sequence words in the box to clarify the order of events in the story. Some sentences do not need sequence words.

after that	afterwards	eventually	first
later	meanwhile	next	soon

Exercise 8 Writing a first draft

GO ONLINE

Review your outline. Then write the first draft of your narrative paragraph about a challenge you faced. Go to the Web to use the Online Writing Tutor.

Exercise 9 Peer editing a first draft

A. After writing a first draft, it is helpful to get feedback on your ideas. Exchange paragraphs with two other people. For each paragraph you read, answer the Peer Editor's Questions on a separate piece of paper. Then discuss your responses.

GO ONLINE

Peer Editor's Questions

1. What is your favorite part of the paragraph?
2. What challenge did the writer face?
3. What questions do you have for the writer?
4. What part of the event can you picture most clearly?
5. Where does the paragraph need more details?

Go to the Web to print out a peer editor's worksheet.

B. Review your feedback and the organization guidelines on page 109. Make notes for your revision. In this step, you may add, remove, or rewrite information to clarify your ideas.

In **Writing Process Step 4** you will . . .

- learn about the simple past.
- learn about past continuous verbs.
- edit your first draft and write a final draft.

Now that you have written a first draft, it is time to edit. When you edit, you make changes that will improve your writing and correct mistakes.

Language and Grammar Focus

GO ONLINE

The Simple Past

Use the simple past to tell about actions and events that started and finished in the past.

Dalia **walked** home quickly that night.
Ronaldo **studied** all night for that exam.

Forming the Simple Past

Add *-d* or *-ed* to the base form of most regular verbs to form the simple past.

In 2003, I **celebrated** Ramadan with my family in Beirut.
I **graduated** from high school in 2001.

Some verbs are irregular in the simple past.

Elizabeth and her sister **spent** all their money.
I **met** my husband at the airport on New Year's Day.

To form a negative statement in the simple past, use *did not* followed by the base form of the verb.

I **did not fall** off the cliff.
I **did not waste** any money.

The verb *be* has two past forms: *was* and *were*.

Waleed **was** a good father.
Scott and Eric **were** anxious.

To form negative statements with *be* in the simple past, use *not* after *was* or *were*.

Ling **was not** nervous.
They **were not** generous people.

AFFIRMATIVE STATEMENTS		
SUBJECT	BASE FORM OF VERB + *-D*/*-ED*	
I You He She It We They	**waited**	patiently.

NEGATIVE STATEMENTS			
SUBJECT	*DID* + *NOT*	BASE FORM OF VERB	
I You He She It We They	**did not**	**wait**	patiently.

AFFIRMATIVE STATEMENTS		
SUBJECT	*WAS/WERE*	
I	**was**	beautiful.
You	**were**	
He She It	**was**	
We You They	**were**	

NEGATIVE STATEMENTS		
SUBJECT	*WAS/WERE + NOT*	
I	**was not**	beautiful.
You	**were not**	
He She It	**was not**	
We You They	**were not**	

Exercise 1 Using verbs in the simple past

Complete the following sentences with verbs in the simple past.

1. I ____was____ interested in astronomy.
2. We ______________ about our plans.
3. Fernando ______________ an umbrella, some sandwiches, and a thermos of hot, sweet tea.
4. My sister and I ______________ for help, and a helicopter ______________ to rescue us.
5. I ______________ the roasted lamb with a salad and some rice.
6. There ______________ 122 people at the wedding.
7. After Hiroshi ______________ his host family, he ______________ less worried.
8. The women ______________ to the top of a mountain where they ______________ a lot of fresh snow.
9. Magdalena ______________ to Zacatecas where she ______________ her grandmother.
10. We ______________ so thirsty that we ______________ three bottles of water.
11. The police ______________ us for speeding in a school zone.
12. The crowd ______________ loudly after the band ______________ their famous song.

Exercise 2 Editing a paragraph

Read and edit the paragraph. Correct mistakes with the simple past. There are nine more mistakes.

> Two years ago, my friends and I ~~decide~~ decided to hike a mountain in my country. We wake up very early in the morning that day. We brought some fruit and drinks for breakfast. After we ate our fruit, we want to climb the mountain. We got to the top at about 10:00 a.m. It was very beautiful. We stay there and talked, but after a while, we wanted to hike some more. We did not brought food, but we had some water, and we started climbing another mountain. We become tired, but we did not wanted to stop. We was thirsty, too, but we did not had enough water. Finally, we met some people, and they gave us drinks and helped us. That day, I learn to be very careful when I go hiking in the mountains.

Language and Grammar Focus

GO ONLINE

The Past Continuous

Use the **past continuous** to describe an event that was already in progress when another event occurred or interrupted the first event.

My brother and I **were watching** TV when we heard a crash.
The car **was moving** slowly, so I had plenty of time to cross the street.

Use the past continuous to tell about two or more activities that were in progress at the same time.

She **was running** while **talking** on the cell phone.
Some teenagers **were splashing** and **shouting** at each other.

Forming the Past Continuous

To form the past continuous, use *was* or *were* and the base form of the verb + *–ing*.

I **was living** in Riyadh at the time.

To form negative statements in the past continuous, use *not* between *was* or *were* and the verb + *–ing*.

We **were not laughing** at the comedian's jokes.

> **!** English speakers do not usually use stative verbs (*be, know, understand, see, believe*) in the past continuous. Use the simple past instead.

AFFIRMATIVE STATEMENTS		
SUBJECT	*WAS/WERE*	BASE FORM OF VERB + *-ING*
I	**was**	**watching.**
You	**were**	
He She It	**was**	
We	**were**	
You		
They		

NEGATIVE STATEMENTS		
SUBJECT	*WAS/WERE* + *NOT*	BASE FORM OF VERB + *-ING*
I	**was not**	**watching.**
You	**were not**	
He She It	**was not**	
We	**were not**	
You		
They		

Exercise 3 Using the past continuous

Answer the following questions with sentences that use the past continuous.

1. What were you doing yesterday at this time?

   I was shopping for a gift for my sister.

2. What were you doing last night at 6:00 p.m.?

   ____

3. What were you doing this morning at 10:00 a.m.?

   ____

4. What were you doing last year at this time?

   ____

5. What were you thinking about while you were coming to school today?

   ____

Exercise 4 Identifying when to use the past continuous

Underline the verbs in each sentence. Then rewrite the sentences replacing the simple past with the past continuous where it is more appropriate.

1. I talked to my friend when the phone died.

   I was talking to my friend when the phone died.

2. I lived in Bogotá when I had a terrible car accident.

   ____

   ____

3. I worked on my paper and watched the game when he called.

____

____

4. A stranger stood in the doorway when we arrived home.

____

____

5. We drove to the hospital when my wife told the taxi driver to stop the car.

____

____

6. In those days I worked and went to school, so I didn't have much free time.

____

____

Exercise 5 Editing a paragraph

Read and edit the paragraph. There are eight more mistakes in simple past and past continuous.

About two years ago, I enrolled in a scuba diving course. My scuba diving teacher ~~was having~~ had a big surprise: I wasn't knowing how to swim. In fact, I was afraid of water. When I was a child, my parents tried to help me, so they make me take many swimming courses. Although I try hard, I did not learning to swim. When I enrolled in the scuba diving course, I was still afraid of water. Every day when I entered the swimming pool, I battle with my fear. Fortunately, my courage won every time. Finally, one day while I practicing my dive, I realized that I was do very well. After six months of hard work, I completed the course. It is true that I was always the worst of the group, but in my own evaluation, I was a champion. I conquer my fear of water. For me, this experience was very important. It was a test of courage, and I passed it.

Exercise 6 Editing your first draft and rewriting

Review your paragraph for mistakes. Use the checklist below. Then write a final draft. Go to the Web to use the Online Writing Tutor.

Editor's Checklist

Put a check (✓) as appropriate.

CONTENT AND ORGANIZATION

○ 1. Does your topic sentence introduce the challenge you faced?

○ 2. Does your paragraph include background information about what happened and who was involved?

○ 3. Does your paragraph include details of what you heard, saw, felt, smelled, or tasted during the experience?

○ 4. Does your concluding sentence explain what you learned from the experience?

LANGUAGE

○ 5. Did you use the simple past to express events that started and finished in the past?

○ 6. Did you check for correct irregular verb forms?

○ 7. Did you use the past continuous to show simultaneous or interrupted actions?

○ 8. Did you capitalize the first letter of each sentence and use end punctuation?

Go to the Web to print out a peer editor's worksheet.

In **Review** you will . . .

- review sensory and emotional details.
- practice recognizing order of events.
- edit for the simple past and past continuous in writing.

In Putting It All Together, you will review what you learned in this unit.

Exercise 1 Identifying sensory and emotional details

Read the sentences below. Write *S* next to the sentences that include sensory details. Write *E* next to the sentences that include emotional details.

_____ 1. Olivia reached for the doorknob, and it was burning hot.

_____ 2. Ibrahim and I arrived around 8:00, and we were happy to be home.

_____ 3. We were greeted by a large man with long, black hair.

_____ 4. I was shocked and disappointed by the results.

_____ 5. My mother always smelled like flowery perfume.

_____ 6. The news left us saddened and worried about the future.

Exercise 2 Identifying order of events

Read the following sentences. Then number them in the order you think they occurred. Use the sequence words and phrases as clues.

__1__ a. For years, I did not know what to do with my life, but after I decided to become a helicopter pilot, I became very dedicated to my goal.

_____ b. To raise money, I delivered groceries in my truck.

_____ c. After I got my visa, I prepared to come to Canada.

_____ d. As a truck driver, I drove all over Japan for five years.

_____ e. First, I did some research and found out that it would cost a lot of money.

_____ f. Once I raised enough money, I was ready to take my training. Someone advised me to do a program in Canada because it was not as expensive, so I decided to come here even though I needed more English.

_____ g. Now, I am in Canada. I go to school to study English. At the same time, I take flying lessons.

_____ h. Later, I got another job delivering fuel to gas stations. I lived in my truck to save money.

_____ i. Finally, I am learning to pilot a helicopter, and soon I will be ready to fly solo. I know that I will reach my goal in two years.

Exercise 3 Editing a paragraph

Read and edit the paragraph. There are ten mistakes in the simple past and past continuous.

Facing Danger in French Guiana

Three years ago, I was living in an exciting and adventurous place: French Guiana. My husband and I own a lovely house that was right next to the jungle. Many animals lived there, such as crocodiles, monkeys, poisonous spiders, jaguars, tigers, and snakes. People often warn us that our house was too close to the jungle, but we enjoying the house so much that we decided to stay. Then one morning I had a frightening adventure. I was plan to go for a swim in the pool. I put on my swimsuit, went outside, and start to cross the patio. I was take off my jacket to dive into the water when suddenly, I had a big surprise. A big snake was swim in my pool and move quickly toward me. I could not breathe. It seemed as though it staring at me for a long time. I ran into the house to call the police. When they arrive, the snake was gone. That day I learned to never jump into that pool before inspecting it for visitors.

In **Timed Writing** you will . . .

- practice writing with a time limit.

Practice your test-taking skills with the following practice topic. Read the prompt. Then follow the steps below.

> **Write a narrative paragraph. Tell about something that happened to you during a trip. Use details to help your readers understand what you experienced and how you felt.**

Step 1 BRAINSTORMING: 5 minutes

Make a list of recent trips you have taken. Write down some of the things you did on those trips, people you met, and things you saw. Add to your list until you decide on a specific incident you would like to write about.

Step 2 OUTLINING: 5 minutes

Fill in the chart with ideas for your writing. Use a separate piece of paper if necessary.

Topic Sentence	
Topic Sentence and Controlling Idea Tell what the story was about and where it took place.	
Supporting Sentences	
First Event Tell what happened first. Use sensory or emotional details.	
Second Event Tell what happened next. Use sensory or emotional details.	
Next Event Tell what else happened. Use sensory or emotional details.	
Last Event Tell how the experience ended. Use sensory or emotional details.	
Concluding Sentence	
Wrap Up Tell why the story was important or what you learned.	

Step 3 **WRITING:** 25 minutes

Use your brainstorming notes and outline to write your paragraph on a separate piece of paper.

Step 4 **EDITING:** 10 minutes

When you have finished your paragraph, check it for mistakes. Use the checklist below.

GO ONLINE

Editor's Checklist

Put a check (✓) as appropriate.

- ○ 1. Does the paragraph have a title?
- ○ 2. Does the topic sentence tell what the story will be about?
- ○ 3. Does the paragraph have background information?
- ○ 4. Does the paragraph give the events of the story?
- ○ 5. Are there sensory and/or emotional details?
- ○ 6. Does the paragraph use sequence words to show the order of events?
- ○ 7. Did you use simple past and past continuous verbs in the correct form?
- ○ 8. Does your conclusion show why the story was important?

Go to the Web to print out a peer editor's worksheet.

Test-Taking Tip

To check that your narrative is complete, be sure to include the three "F"s: **Facts** (what happened), **Feelings** (how the people in the story felt), and **Future** (how the events might affect people in the future).

Topics for Future Writing

Write a narrative paragraph on one of the following topics.

Education: How do people learn? In answering this question, tell the story of a person who learned a significant lesson. How did he or she learn it? How did the experience change the person?

Geology/Geography: Tell the story of a particular geological event (e.g., the Ice Age, a volcanic eruption, etc.). What happened? Why was this event significant? How did it change the place where the event occurred? How did it affect other places in the world?

Health Sciences: Tell the story of how a treatment for a particular disease was discovered and how it has progressed over the years. In the past, did everyone agree on how the disease should be treated? Why or why not? What happened to change people's opinions? Who discovered the treatment?

History: Tell the story of an important historical event. What happened? Who was involved? Why was the event important? What happened before and after the event?

Nursing: Describe a typical day for a nurse. What are the responsibilities of a nurse? How does the nurse take care of patients? With whom does the nurse interact?

UNIT 6

Opinion Paragraphs

Academic Focus Urban Studies

Unit Goals

Rhetorical Focus

- opinion organization
- reasons to support an opinion

Language and Grammar Focus

- *there is* and *there are* to introduce facts
- *because of* and *because* to give reasons

In an opinion paragraph, the writer expresses and supports an opinion on a particular topic or issue. The writer must give reasons that help persuade the reader to agree with him or her.

Exercise 1 Thinking about the topic

Discuss the picture with a partner.

- Describe the picture.
- What do you like about the city in the picture?
- Would you like to live in a place like this? Why or why not?
- How does this place compare with the city or town where you live?
- Have you ever visited a city like the one in the photo? Describe your experience.

Exercise 2 Reading about the topic

Urban studies professionals study city life, government, and community services. The writer of this article explains the characteristics of a healthy city. What does the author mean by "healthy city"?

A Healthy City

Recently there have been a number of studies to determine what makes for a healthy city. The studies have led to a movement to improve city life. The following are city **features** suggested by the healthy city movement.

1. Public transportation: With public transportation, people do not have to drive their cars everywhere, and businesses do not need to provide as much parking. Public transportation encourages people to walk and get more exercise. With fewer cars on roads, cities with public transportation have better air quality. There is less pollution and less traffic in healthy cities.
2. **Diverse** neighborhoods. Neighborhoods with diverse populations encourage people to get to know each other. People learn about different ethnicities, and they respect each other. People in diverse communities learn to appreciate people with different skills, interests, and abilities.
3. Trees, gardens, and parks. Trees add to the beauty of a city and provide shade in hot summers. They also help clean the air. Community gardens bring people together and provide **nutritious** food. People can save money by growing their own food. They can also share what they grow or sell it for income. Community parks also improve life in cities. They provide places for people to meet and for children to play.

features: characteristics
diverse: mixed ethnically, in gender, or in income
nutritious: full of vitamins and minerals

Exercise 3 Understanding the text

Write *T* for true or *F* for false for each statement.

_____ 1. Public transportation creates a healthy city because it improves air quality.

_____ 2. In a diverse community, people develop closer relationships.

_____ 3. Community gardens are bad for business because people grow their food rather than buy it.

_____ 4. A healthy city encourages healthy eating and exercise.

Exercise 4 Responding to the text

Answer the following questions about the reading.

1. According to the writer, why is public transportation important?

____

2. Does your hometown have any of the characteristics of a healthy city? Which?

____

3. What else would you add to the features of a healthy city?

____

Exercise 5 Freewriting

Write for ten minutes in your journal. Choose from topics below or an idea of your own. Express your thoughts and feelings. Don't worry about mistakes.

- Explain which feature of a healthy city is most important to you.
- What is your favorite city? Why?
- What would you change about the place where you live?
- In what ways can people living in a big city protect the environment?

In **Writing Process Step 2** you will . . .

- learn about opinion organization.
- brainstorm ideas and specific vocabulary to use in your writing.
- determine the audience and purpose for your opinion paragraph.
- create an outline for your paragraph.

Writing Process Step 2 | Brainstorming and Outlining

WRITING TASK In this unit, you will write an opinion paragraph about a city or town that you think provides a good quality of life. Give reasons for why you believe the place is a good place to live. Go to the Web to use the Online Writing Tutor.

Exercise 1 Brainstorming ideas

A. Put a check (✓) in the column for the features that support each topic below. Some features may support more than one topic.

	TOPICS		
FEATURES OF A CITY	A Family City	A City of Opportunities	A Tourist City
Entertainment			
Weather & Air Quality			
Job and Educational Opportunities			
Safety			
Shopping			
Cultural Attractions			
Affordability			
Natural Beauty (parks, lakes, beaches, trees)			
Medical Facilities			
Public Transportation			
Other: ______________			

B. Select three to five features that are most important to include in your opinion paragraph.

____

____

____

____

Exercise 2 Identifying audience and purpose

A. Think about the audience and purpose for your paragraph by answering the questions below.

1. Who might be interested in your topic? (Choose one.)
   a. tourists planning to visit the city
   b. companies looking for a city to open offices or to hold a convention
   c. people deciding on a city to move to
2. Why might they be reading your paragraph? (Choose one.)
   a. entertainment
   b. advice
   c. information
3. Where would you most likely see a paragraph like yours? (Choose one.)
   a. in a travel magazine
   b. in a business journal
   c. in a brochure for tourists
4. What do you expect your reader to do after reading your paragraph? (Choose one.)
   a. visit my city
   b. learn about my city
   c. live in my city

B. On a separate piece of paper, write about the audience and purpose for your paragraph.

Exercise 3 Brainstorming vocabulary

A. Add vocabulary expressions for each feature.

Entertainment: ______________________________

Jobs and Education: ______________________________

Safety: ______________________________

Shopping: ______________________________

Tourist Attractions: ______________________________

Natural Beauty: ______________________________

Public Transportation: ______________________________

B. Match the adjective on the left with a noun on the right.

1. __*j*__ historic		a. architeture
2. _____ lush		b. climate
3. _____ tree-lined		c. districts
4. _____ public		d. neighborhoods
5. _____ colonial		e. restaurants
6. _____ a mild		f. squares
7. _____ friendly		g. vegetation
8. _____ shopping		h. boulevards
9. _____ gourmet		i. hotels
10. _____ successful		j. monuments
11. _____ luxury		k. companies

C. Use vocabulary from Part A or Part B to write five sentences for your paragraph.

____

____

____

____

Rhetorical Focus

Opinion Organization

In an opinion paragraph, the writer presents an opinion and tries to persuade readers to agree with the opinion.

Topic Sentence

- The topic sentence introduces the topic and states the writer's opinion.

Supporting Sentences

- The middle sentences give reasons that support the writer's opinion.
- Writers often use facts, explanations, and personal experiences to support their opinions.

Concluding Sentence

- The last sentence restates the writer's opinion in different words.
- It also comments on the opinion in some way.
- The concluding sentence sometimes asks readers to take some action.

Exercise 4 Reading a student paragraph

Read the paragraph. Why does the writer like St. Petersburg?

St. Petersburg

My favorite city to live in is St. Petersburg, Russia. It is true that it has long, cold winters, but I still like the city for many reasons. First, it has beautiful architecture. The city was built during the reign of Peter the Great, and there are many buildings of that period in different parts of the city. The most amazing architecture can be found in the city's numerous palaces. In addition, the city has great museums. Two examples are the State Hermitage and the Russian Museum. The Hermitage contains works by Picasso, Matisse, and Monet. The third attraction of the city is its walking culture. You can find people walking at any time of the day or night. People walk for pleasure, or they walk to a shop, restaurant, or work. Because of this walking culture, most people dress in nice clothes. Finally, St. Petersburg has many types of public transportation. There are underground trains, trolleys, and buses that go everywhere in the city. As a result, people do not have to have a car, and there is little traffic in most parts of the city. Whether you live in St. Petersburg or just visit, it is a fantastic place to be.

Exercise 5 Examining the student paragraph

A. Answer the following questions about the student paragraph.

1. What do you think is St. Petersburg's best quality?

   ____

2. What else would you like to know about St. Petersburg?

   ____

3. If you could, would you like to live in St. Petersburg? Why or why not?

   ____

4. How does your city compare to St. Petersburg?

   ____

B. Examine the organization of the paragraph. Respond to the questions and statements below. Compare answers with a partner.

1. Circle the topic sentence.
2. Which one of the following reasons is NOT included in the paragraph?
   a. public transportation
   b. safety
   c. architecture
   d. walking culture
3. Underline the concluding sentence twice. The concluding sentence gives—
   a. a summary of the main reasons.
   b. a suggestion that the reader visit St. Petersburg.
   c. a final comment about the city.

Exercise 6 Writing an outline

GO ONLINE

Review your brainstorming ideas and the information on opinion organization. Then go to the Web to print out an outline template for your paragraph.

In **Writing Process Step 3** you will . . .

- learn to use facts, explanations, and experiences to support opinions.
- write a first draft of your opinion paragraph.

Exercise 1 Reading a student paragraph

Read the paragraph. Why is Da Lat a paradise?

A Vietnamese Paradise

In Vietnam, the best place to spend a honeymoon is the beautiful mountain city Da Lat. First of all, the city has a pleasant climate all year round because it is high above the ocean. Sometimes fog comes in, and the city becomes mysterious and private. At other times, the sun shines, and Da Lat is cheerful and lively. There are beautiful gardens and lovely French colonial architecture. Second, young couples can walk along the boulevards in the shade of tall pine trees. They can sit on benches in the flower parks. In addition, Da Lat has many facilities for visitors. There are excellent hotels that have special rooms with candles and beautiful decorations for honeymooners. Also, the city has many things to do at night. Newlyweds can go out to one of the stylish restaurants that are open late. The lights are soft, and the music is romantic. The newlyweds can eat delicious food, listen to music, and meet other young couples. Da Lat is the Vietnamese people's first choice for a honeymoon because it has a pleasant climate, many beautiful places to visit, and good hotels and restaurants.

Exercise 2 Examining the student paragraph

A. Answer the following questions about the student paragraph. Use a separate piece of paper.

1. What makes Da Lat a perfect destination for a couple going on a honeymoon?
2. What other information do you need about Da Lat to decide whether to spend a honeymoon there?
3. What features does the writer think are important in a city for honeymooners?

B. Examine the organization of the paragraph. Respond to the questions and statements below. Compare answers with a partner.

1. Circle the topic sentence. Which statement best describes the main idea of the paragraph? (Choose one.)
   a. Da Lat is the perfect place to have a honeymoon.
   b. Da Lat is a perfect place for visitors.
   c. Vietnam is a paradise on Earth.
2. How many reasons does the writer include? ____________________
3. Which of the following reasons does the author use to support her opinion? (Choose all that apply.)
   a. the climate
   b. the scenery and architecture
   c. the nightlife
   d. the transportation
4. Underline the concluding sentence twice. The concluding sentence gives—
   a. a suggestion that the reader should have a honeymoon in Da Lat.
   b. a promise that Da Lat will not disappoint the reader.
   c. a summary of the main reasons why Da Lat is a great place for a honeymoon.

Rhetorical Focus

Using Reasons to Support an Opinion

There are often many different opinions about a certain topic. Therefore, writers must give reasons for their opinions to convince their readers. They often come up with reasons by asking themselves, *How do you know?*

These supporting reasons are often in the form of facts, explanations, or experiences.

A **fact** is a piece of information that people generally agree is true. In an opinion paragraph, a writer might use scientific, historical, or other types of facts.

Winters in Prague are very cold.

An **explanation** cannot be proven (like a fact can), but it still helps the reader understand why the writer holds a certain opinion.

It is not easy to deal with those cold, windy days.

An **experience** is something that happened to the writer or someone else. Writers often use experiences to show how they were influenced to think a certain way.

My cousin once got frostbite while waiting at a bus stop.

Exercise 3 Identifying facts, explanations, and experiences

Read each opinion and the reasons that support it. Write *fact*, *explanation*, or *experience* next to each reason.

1. Tokyo is the most technologically advanced city in Asia.

    ___fact___ a. In Tokyo, most people have cell phones, and many buildings are equipped with wireless technology.

    ________ b. People's daily lives come to a halt if there is a blackout in Tokyo.

    ________ c. I rode the subway in Tokyo for many years, and it never broke down.

    ________ d. Some subway stations in Tokyo can handle more than a million passengers a day because of the use of computers.

2. Hawaii has the best surfing beaches in the United States.

    ________ a. If you have never surfed in the Hawaiian Islands, you cannot be a world-class surfer because Hawaii is the benchmark by which other beaches are evaluated.

    ________ b. The winter waves in Oahu are higher than the summer waves, so serious surfers tend to spend time there during the winter months.

    ________ c. I have been surfing all over the world, but I still prefer surfing in Hawaii.

    ________ d. Storm waves can rise as high as 20 feet with a face of up to 50 feet.

3. There is no better city to visit than Istanbul.

    ________ a. People in Istanbul are friendly and always willing to help their neighbors.

    ________ b. Both women and men can visit the beautiful Blue Mosque in the city's historic area.

    ________ c. I had the best meal of my life in a small café in Istanbul.

    ________ d. Istanbul has a historically important location as a port city on the only route between the Mediterranean and the Black Sea.

Exercise 4 Using reasons to support an opinion

Complete each sentence with the name of a city or place that you know. Then support your opinion by answering the question "How do you know?" with a fact, explanation, or experience.

1. ___Chicago___ has a high cost of living.

   How do you know?

   Fact: A simple one-bedroom apartment in the city is over $1,000 a month, compared to about $500 in many other big U.S. cities.

   Explanation: People sometimes work more than one job in Chicago just to afford a small apartment.

   Experience: My cousin is an engineer with a good job in Chicago, but he still cannot afford to live in the city, so he lives in the suburbs of Chicago.

2. ______________ has the most beautiful beaches.

   How do you know?

   Fact: ______________________________

   Explanation: ______________________________

   Experience: ______________________________

3. ______________ is the most popular tourist destination in my country.

   How do you know?

   Fact: ______________________________

   Explanation: ______________________________

   Experience: ______________________________

4. ______________ is a great place to raise a family.

   How do you know?

   Fact: ______________________________

   Explanation: ______________________________

   Experience: ______________________________

Exercise 5 Writing a first draft

GO ONLINE

Review your outline. Then write the first draft of your opinion paragraph about a city or town that you think provides a good quality of life. Go to the Web to use the Online Writing Tutor.

Exercise 6 Peer editing a first draft

A. After writing a first draft, it is helpful to get feedback on your ideas. Exchange paragraphs with two other people. For each paragraph you read, answer the Peer Editor's Questions on a separate piece of paper. Then discuss your responses.

GO ONLINE

Peer Editor's Questions

1. What is your favorite part of the paragraph?
2. Who do you think will be interested in reading this paragraph? Why?
3. What is the writer's opinion?
4. What facts, explanations, or experiences does the writer use to support the opinion?
5. What questions do you have for the writer?

Go to the Web to print out a peer editor's worksheet.

B. Review your feedback and the organization guidelines on page 137. Make notes for your revision. In this step, you may add, remove, or rewrite information to clarify your ideas.

- learn how to use *there is* and *there are* in statements.
- learn how to use *because of* or *because* to give reasons.
- edit your first draft and write a final draft.

Now that you have written a first draft, it is time to edit. When you edit, you make changes that will improve your writing and correct mistakes.

Language and Grammar Focus

GO ONLINE

Using *There Is* and *There Are*

Writers often use *there is* or *there are* to introduce facts.

There are harvest festivals every autumn.

There is a picturesque village in the mountains near La Paz.

There are no mosquitoes at this altitude.

In a statement, a noun or a noun phrase follows *there is* or *there are.* Use *there are* with plural nouns. Use *there is* with all other nouns.

There are tall trees lining the street in Taipei. (plural noun)

There is a large lake near Maracaibo. (singular noun)

There is water beyond the mountains. (noncount noun)

Use *no* after *there is* or *there are* to express a negative fact.

There is **no** snow.

There are **no** theaters in my hometown.

Exercise 1 Practicing with *there is* and *there are*

Write *is* or *are* in the blanks to complete the sentences below.

1. There __is__ a parade of children holding flowers.
2. There _______ a lot of music in the streets.
3. There _______ many restaurants.
4. There _______ not many cars on the road, but you might see bicycles.
5. There _______ no airport in my city.
6. There _______ not much wind, so people prefer this beach.
7. There _______ many tourist attractions in Barcelona.

Exercise 2 Writing sentences with *there is* and *there are*

Rewrite the following sentences using *there is* or *there are*.

1. Bad weather is not in the South.

   There is no bad weather in the South.
2. Houses are not on the island.

   ____
3. Colorful birds are in the jungle.

   ____
4. Many international restaurants are downtown.

   ____
5. Many vendors are on the beach.

   ____

Language and Grammar Focus

Using *Because of* and *Because*

Use *because* or *because of* to give a reason. *Because of* is followed by a noun phrase.

People spend a lot of time outdoors **because of** the mild climate.

Because is followed by a complete sentence with its own subject and verb.

Tourists are attracted to the coast **because** the fishing is fantastic.

Note that in each example, *because of* and *because* give a reason after a statement.

Because of and *because* can also appear before the statement. When they come before, use a comma.

Because of the mild climate**,** people spend a lot of time outdoors.

Because the fishing is fantastic**,** tourists are attracted to the coast.

Exercise 3 Using *because of* and *because*

Complete each sentence with *because of* or *because.*

1. This city is a good place for young people because of the amusement parks.
2. There is a lot of diversity ____________ many people from Europe and Asia moved to Brazil during the past two centuries.
3. Many people retire to warmer climates ____________ the weather.
4. Gardening is popular there ____________ the valley has ideal conditions for roses.

Exercise 4 Using *because of* and *because*

Finish each sentence with a phrase or a statement of your own.

1. I want to live in a big city because of the cultural life.
2. My city is beautiful because of ______________________________
3. Shanghai is interesting because ______________________________
4. A small town is perfect for a family with children because ______________________________
5. I do not want to live in a big city because of ______________________________

Exercise 5 Editing a paragraph

Read and edit the paragraph. There are five more mistakes with *because/because of* and *there is/there are.*

The Beautiful Faces of Rio de Janeiro

I was very sad when I had to leave Rio de Janeiro because it is the best place on Earth. Naturally, I like this city because ~~of~~ it is my hometown. However, others are fond of Rio, too, for different reasons. First, Rio is well known because its many beautiful people, especially in the beach neighborhoods such as Ipanema. They look especially stunning when they dress up in costumes and dance in the streets. Rio is also popular because its natural beauty. The city is on the Atlantic Ocean. There is a lot of beaches, and they are full of activity every day. You can see great geological formations, such as the granite mountain called Sugar Loaf. On another peak named Corcovado, you can see an enormous statue that looks over the city. Finally, Rio is a popular destination for people who enjoy tranquility. Across the center of the city, in the middle of all the noise, there is the most beautiful botanical gardens filled with exotic varieties of plants and animals. In short, Rio de Janeiro is a popular city because its people, natural beauty, and diverse places to visit.

Exercise 6 Editing your first draft and rewriting

Review your paragraph for mistakes. Use the checklist below. Then write a final draft. Go to the Web to use the Online Writing Tutor.

GO ONLINE

Editor's Checklist

Put a check (✓) as appropriate.

CONTENT AND ORGANIZATION

○ 1. Does your paragraph have a topic sentence?

○ 2. Does your paragraph include several reasons that support your opinion?

○ 3. Did you support your opinion with facts, explanations, or experiences?

○ 4. Does your paragraph have a conclusion?

LANGUAGE

○ 5. Did you use *there is* or *there are* to introduce the existence or location of something or someplace?

○ 6. Did you use *because* to give reasons with statements?

○ 7. Did you use *because of* to give reasons with noun phrases?

Go to the Web to print out a peer editor's worksheet.

In **Review** you will . . .

- review the use of facts, explanations, and experiences to support opinions.
- practice using *there is* and *there are*.
- practice using *because* and *because of* to give reasons.

In Putting It All Together, you will review what you learned in this unit.

Exercise 1 Identifying facts, explanations, and experiences

Read each opinion and the reasons that support it. Write *fact*, *explanation*, or *experience* next to each reason.

1. The Guggenheim Museum is the most interesting building in New York City.

______________________ a. The tilted corkscrew shape of the building is unlike anything else in the city.

______________________ b. It was designed by the American architect Frank Loyd Wright.

______________________ c. The first time I saw the Guggenheim, I was so amazed that I spent an hour just looking at the building from the outside.

______________________ d. Many visitors have trouble focusing on the artwork because they are distracted by the architecture.

2. People spend too much money on personal appearance.

______________________ a. People spend billions annually on cosmetics.

______________________ b. People want to look good, but they are spending money that could be used for more important purposes such as education or a home.

______________________ c. Cosmetic surgery is becoming more and more costly.

______________________ d. My brother-in-law had to work overtime to pay for his wife's clothing and jewelry.

3. Water is our most important natural resource.

______________________ a. What would happen in your house if you lost water for one day?

______________________ b. The human body is 98 percent water.

______________________ c. Lack of fresh drinking water causes major health crises in some countries every year.

______________________ d. Not only is water important for drinking, washing, and bathing, it is also important for growing food.

Exercise 2 Writing sentences with *there is* and *there are*

Rewrite the following sentences with *there is* or *there are*.

1. Whales are off the coast of Salvador Bahia in Brazil during the winter and spring.

 ____

2. Gold exists in China.

 ____

3. Penguins are not in Iran.

 ____

4. No cure exists for cancer.

 ____

5. Many stories exist about the first blue-eyed tribes that lived in Argentina.

 ____

6. Beautiful terraced hillsides are in Afghanistan.

 ____

Exercise 3 Using *because of* and *because*

Complete each sentence with *because of* or *because*.

1. Many people learn English ______________ their jobs.
2. Many young people go out in the evening ______________ they like to listen to music.
3. Our food is hot ______________ we use a lot of chilies.
4. Most people do not have private boats ______________ they are very expensive.
5. We won the game ______________ the other goalie's error.
6. A lot of people become English teachers ______________ the opportunities to travel.

In Timed Writing you will . . .

- practice writing with a time limit.

Practice your test-taking skills with the following practice topic. Read the prompt. Then follow the steps below.

> **Write an opinion paragraph. Express your opinion about what age is best for getting married. Give reasons to support your opinion.**

Step 1 BRAINSTORMING: 5 minutes

Make a list of facts, explanations, and experiences to support one age for getting married. Then choose your best reasons for your paragraph.

Step 2 OUTLINING: 5 minutes

Fill in the chart with ideas for your writing.

Topic Sentence	
Opinion Introduce your topic and state your opinion.	
Supporting Sentences	
Reason 1 Give facts, explanations, or experience to support your opinion.	
Reason 2 Give facts, explanations, or experience to support your opinion.	
Reason 3 Give facts, explanations, or experience to support your opinion.	
Concluding Sentence	
Restatement of Topic Sentence Restate your opinion and provide an extra comment.	

Step 3 WRITING: 25 MINUTES

Use your brainstorming notes and outline to write your paragraph on a separate piece of paper.

Step 4 EDITING: 10 minutes

When you have finished your paragraph, check it for mistakes. Use the checklist below.

GO ONLINE

Editor's Checklist

Put a check (✓) as appropriate.

○ 1. Does the topic sentence state your opinion about the topic?

○ 2. Did you include facts, explanations, and personal experiences to support your opinion?

○ 3. Does your concluding sentence restate your opinion?

○ 4. Did you use *there is* or *there are* to introduce facts?

○ 5. Did you use *because of* and *because* when giving reasons?

○ 6. Did you capitalize the first letter of each sentence and use end punctuation?

Go to the Web to print out a peer editor's worksheet.

Topics for Future Writing

Write an opinion paragraph on one of the following topics.

Biology: Should companies be allowed to test new products such as medicine or beauty products on animals? Why or why not?

Engineering: Should people switch from cars running on gasoline to electric cars? Why or why not?

Marketing: Why do you buy a certain brand of electronics?

Medicine: Who has more responsibility for an individual's health: people or government? Why?

Psychology: What are some possible reasons for lying?

Sociology: In what ways do public parks benefit a neighborhood?

Appendices

Step 1: Stimulating Ideas

Begin writing by gathering ideas. Read your assignment carefully, and make sure you understand the task. Then think about what you already know about the topic.

▶ **Strategies:** Highlight important parts of your assignment. Check your assignment often throughout the process. Talk to classmates about your ideas, and write about them in your journal. Circle the ideas that are the most interesting to you. Then choose one to write about.

Step 2: Brainstorming and Outlining

Make a plan that has a clear focus and a logical sequence. Write in a way that the reader will understand by organizing your controlling idea and supporting details.

▶ **Strategies:** Create a list, diagram, chart, or web. Use it to decide how you will organize your main idea and supporting details. Think about your audience and purpose as you organize. Also make a list of vocabulary words that you will use. Finally, make an outline that will guide the drafting process. Don't forget to check the assignment as you work.

Step 3: Developing Your Ideas

Write a first draft that explains your ideas. Try to follow the outline, and explain the ideas as clearly as you can. You may change your ideas while you write. That is okay because the first draft is one step in a longer process.

▶ **Strategies:** Write your first draft without stopping. Double-space so that you have room to make changes later. When you finish, look at your outline and the assignment again. Then read your work. Take out parts that do not belong. Add explanations and details that will make your writing clearer. Have a peer read your paper and give you feedback.

Step 4: Editing Your Writing

Your second draft gives you the opportunity to clarify your meaning and check grammar, vocabulary, spelling, and punctuation. The final draft should be easy to read and should have no mistakes.

▶ **Strategies:** Use a checklist to look for mistakes in subject-verb agreement, verb tense, singular/plural forms, word forms, word order, and punctuation. Also check a dictionary for any vocabulary or spelling questions you have. Then write a final draft. Make sure this final draft has one-inch margins, is double-spaced, has a title, and lists your name, date, and class on the top of the first page.

Commas (,)

A comma is used to separate information from other parts of the sentence.

1. Use a comma to separate items in a series. Use *and* before the last item if you list three or more items.
   - The region produces wheat**,** corn**,** and rice.
2. Use a comma to separate an introductory word or phrase.
   - On weekends**,** tourists can explore nearby beaches.
3. Use a comma to separate two sentences that are joined by a conjunction such as *and, but,* or *so.*
   - The temperature drops below zero**,** but the river does not freeze.

Periods (.)

Use a period to mark the end of a sentence. Put one space after a period before starting the next sentence.

- She speaks four languages. Now, she is learning a fifth.

Exclamation Marks (!)

Use explanation marks to stress an idea or show strong emotion.

- Sliding across my bare foot was a giant snake!

Question Marks (?)

Use question marks at the end of questions.

- Why would anyone want to jump out of an airplane?

Semicolons (;)

Use a semicolon to join sentences. Sometimes they are used to join separate sentences without a connector word.

- They help each other; Elvira does the bookkeeping while Alyssa takes care of customers.

Use a semicolon when you join two sentences with a connector such as *however* or *therefore.*

- The oceans hold many secrets**; however,** new technology is helping scientists to understand oceans better.

Apostrophes (')

Use an apostrophe to show possession.

1. When a noun is singular, add an apostrophe and *s* to show possession. In this example, there is one minister.

- Tourists can visit the minister's office.

2. When a noun is plural, put the apostrophe after the plural *s*. In this example, there are two or more ministers.

- Tourists can visit the ministers' office.

3. When a noun ends in *s*, you may add the apostrophe + *s* after the final *s*. Alternatively, you can add just the apostrophe.

- Follow the boss's instructions carefully.
- Follow the boss' instructions carefully.

4. Apostrophes also replace a missing letter to form contractions; however, they are not appropriate in academic writing.

- Computers aren't always necessary.

Quotation Marks ("...")

Use quotation marks to show that you are repeating or quoting someone else's words.

Put quotation marks around only the exact words you take from someone else's speech or writing. Use a comma to separate the quote from the rest of the sentence.

- The king said**, "**The happiness and welfare of my people are my first priority.**"**

Capitalization

Capital letters are used at the beginning of sentences.

- **W**e hiked out to a beautiful waterfall.

Capitalize the days of the week and the months of the year.

- Elections are held on the second **T**uesday in **N**ovember.

Capitalize nouns, verbs, and adjectives in the names of places, people, and organizations.

- **M**r. **W**ong is the president of **H**ealthcare **S**olutions in **S**hanghai.

Appendix III | Glossary

Adapted from the *Grammar Sense* Glossary of Grammar Terms

action verb A verb that describes a thing that someone or something does. An action verb does not describe a state or condition.

Tomoko **rang** the bell.

It **rains** a lot here.

active sentence In active sentences, the agent (the noun that is performing the action) is in subject position, and the receiver (the noun that receives or is a result of the action) is in object position. In the following sentence, the subject *Alex* performed the action, and the object *letter* received the action.

Alex mailed the letter.

adjective A word that describes or modifies the meaning of a noun.

the **orange** car   a **strange** noise

adverb A word that describes or modifies the meaning of a verb, another adverb, an adjective, or a sentence. Many adverbs answer such questions as *How? When? Where? or How often?* They often end in *–ly*.

She ran **quickly**.   She ran **very** quickly.
a **really** hot day   **Maybe** she will leave.

adverbial phrase A phrase that functions as an adverb.

Fatima spoke **very softly.**

affirmative statement A sentence that does not have a negative verb.

Mariana went to the movies.

agreement The subject and verb of a clause must agree in number. If the subject is singular, the verb form is also singular. If the subject is plural, the verb form is also plural.

He comes home early.

They come home early.

article The words *a, an,* and *the* in English. Articles are used to introduce and identify nouns.

a potato   **an** onion   **the** supermarket

auxiliary verb A verb that is used before main verbs (or other auxiliary verbs) in a sentence. Auxiliary verbs are usually used in questions and negative sentences. *Do, have,* and *be* can act as auxiliary verbs. Modals (*may, can, will*) are also auxiliary verbs.

Do you have the time?
The car **was** speeding.
I **have** never been to Italy.
I **may** be late.

base form The form of a verb without any verb endings; the infinitive form without *to.*

sleep   be   stop

clause A group of words that has a subject and a verb. *See also* **dependent clause** and **main clause.**

If I leave, ... when he speaks.
The rain stopped.   . . . that I saw.

common noun A noun that refers to any of a class of people, animals, places, things, or ideas. Common nouns are not capitalized.

man   cat   city   pencil   grammar

comparative A form of an adjective, adverb, or noun that is used to express differences between two items or situations.

This book is **heavier than** that one.
He runs **more quickly than** his brother.
A laptop costs **more money than** a tablet.

complex sentence A sentence that has a main clause and one or more dependent clauses.

When the bell rang, we were finishing dinner.

compound sentence A sentence that has two main clauses separated by a comma and a conjunction, or by a semicolon.

She is very talented; she can sing and dance.

conditional sentence A sentence that expresses a real or unreal situation in the *if* clause, and the (real or unreal) expected result in the main clause.

If I have time, I will travel to Australia.
If I had time, I would travel to Australia.

count noun A common noun that can be counted. It usually has both a singular and a plural form.

orange — oranges   woman — women

definite article The word *the* in English. It is used to identify nouns based on assumptions about what information the speaker and listener share about the noun. The definite article is also used for making general statements about a whole class or group of nouns.

Please give me **the** key.
The scorpion is dangerous.

dependent clause A clause that cannot stand alone as a sentence because it depends on the main clause to complete the meaning of the sentence. Also called *subordinate clause.*

I am going home **after he calls**.

determiner A word such as *a, an, the, this, that, these, those, my, some, a few,* and all numbers that are used before a noun to limit its meaning in some way.

those DVDs

future A time that is to come. The future is expressed in English with *will, be going to,* the simple present, or the present continuous. These different forms of the future often have different meanings and uses.

I **will** help you later.
Ahmed **is going to** call later.
The train **leaves** at 6:05 this evening.
I**'m driving to** Baghdad tomorrow.

gerund An *-ing* form of a verb that is used in place of a noun or pronoun to name an activity or a state.

Skiing is fun. He doesn't like **being sick**.

***if* clause** A dependent clause that begins with *if* and expresses a real or unreal situation.

If I have the time, I will paint the kitchen.
If I had the time, I would paint the kitchen.

indefinite article The words *a* and *an* in English. Indefinite articles introduce a noun as a member of a class of nouns or make generalizations about a whole class or group of nouns.

An ocean is **a** large body of water.

independent clause *See* **main clause.**

indirect object A noun or pronoun used after some verbs that refers to the person who receives the direct object of a sentence.

Feng wrote a letter to **Mei**.
Please buy some milk for **us**.

infinitive A verb form that includes *to* + the base form of a verb. An infinitive is used in place of a noun or pronoun to name an activity or situation expressed by a verb.

Do you like **to swim**?

intransitive verb A verb that cannot be followed by an object.

We finally **arrived**.

main clause A clause that can be used by itself as a sentence. Also called *independent clause.*

I am going home.

main verb A verb that can be used alone in a sentence. A main verb can also occur with an auxiliary verb.

I **ate** lunch at 11:30.
Kate cannot **eat** lunch today.

modal The auxiliary verbs *can, could, may, might, must, should, will,* and *would.* They modify the meaning of a main verb by expressing ability, authority, formality, politeness, or various degrees of certainty. Also called *modal auxiliary.*

You **should** take something for your headache.
Applicants **must** have a high school diploma.

negative statement A sentence with a negative verb.

I **did not see** that movie.

noun A word that typically refers to a person, animal, place, thing, or idea.

Tom rabbit store computer mathematics

noun clause A dependent clause that can occur in the same place as a noun, pronoun, or noun phrase in a sentence. Noun clauses begin with *wh-* words, *if, whether,* or *that.*

I don't know **where he is**.
I wonder **if he is coming**.
I don't know **whether it is true**.
I think **that it is a lie**.

noun phrase A phrase formed by a noun and its modifiers. A noun phrase can substitute for a noun in a sentence.

She drank **milk**.
She drank **chocolate milk**.
She drank **the milk**.

object A noun, pronoun, or noun phrase that follows a transitive verb or a preposition.

He likes **pizza**. Go with **her**.
She likes **ham**. Truong threw **the ball**.

passive sentence Passive sentences emphasize the receiver of an action by changing the usual order of the subject and object in a sentence. In the sentence below, the subject *(The letter)* does not perform the action; it receives the action or is the result of an action. The passive is formed with a form of *be* + the past participle of a transitive verb.

The letter was mailed yesterday.

past continuous A verb form that expresses an action or situation in progress at a specific time in the past. The past continuous is formed with *was* or *were* + verb + *-ing.* Also called *past progressive.*

A: What **were** you **doing** last night at eight o'clock?

B: I **was studying**.

past participle A past verb form that may differ from the simple past form of some irregular verbs. It is used to form the present perfect.

I have never **seen** that movie.

phrasal verb A two- or three-word verb such as *turn down* or *run out of.* The meaning of a phrasal verb is usually different from the meanings of its individual words.

She **turned down** the job offer.
Do not **run out of gas** on the freeway.

phrase A group of words that can form a grammatical unit. A phrase can take the form of a noun phrase, verb phrase, adjective phrase, adverbial phrase, or prepositional phrase. This means it can act as a noun, verb, adjective, adverb, or preposition.

The **tall man** left. She spoke **too fast**.
Lee **hit the ball**. They ran **down the stairs.**

preposition A word such as *at, in, on,* or *to,* that links nouns, pronouns, and gerunds to other words.

prepositional phrase A phrase that consists of a preposition followed by a noun or noun phrase.

on Tuesday under the table

present continuous A verb form that indicates that an activity is in progress, temporary, or changing. It is formed with *be* + verb + *-ing.* Also called *present progressive.*

I **am watering** the garden.
Kelly **is working** for her uncle.

present perfect A verb form that expresses a connection between the past and the present. It indicates indefinite past time, recent past time, or continuing past time. The present perfect is formed with *have* + the past participle of the main verb.

I **have seen** that movie.
The manager **has** just **resigned**.
We **have been** here for three hours.

pronoun A word that can replace a noun or noun phrase. *I, you, he, she, it, mine,* and *yours* are some examples of pronouns.

quantity expression A word or words that occur before a noun to express a quantity or amount of that noun.

a lot of rain **few** books **four** trucks

simple past A verb form that expresses actions and situations that were completed at a definite time in the past.

Bahar **ate** lunch. She **was** hungry.

simple present A verb form that expresses general statements, especially about habitual or repeated activities and permanent situations.

Every morning I **catch** the 8:00 bus.
The moon **is** round.

stative verb A type of verb that is not usually used in the continuous form because it expresses a condition or state that is not changing. *Know, love, see,* and *smell* are some examples.

subject A noun, pronoun, or noun phrase that precedes the verb phrase in a sentence. The subject is closely related to the verb as the doer or experiencer of the action or state, or closely related to the noun that is being described in a sentence with *be.*

Jessica kicked the ball.
The park is huge.

subordinate clause *See* **dependent clause.**

superlative A form of an adjective, adverb, or noun that is used to rank an item or situation first or last in a group of three or more.

This perfume has **the strongest** scent.
He speaks **the fastest** of all.
That machine makes **the most noise** of the three.

tense The form of a verb that shows past, present, and future time.

He **lives** in Kabul now.
He **lived** in Caracas two years ago.
He **will live** in New Delhi next year.

time clause A dependent clause that begins with a word such as *while, when, before,* or *after.* It expresses the relationship in time between two different events in the same sentence.

Before Stephanie left, she fixed the copy machine.

time expression A phrase that functions as an adverb of time.

She graduated **three years ago**.
I will see them **the day after tomorrow**.

transitive verb A verb that is followed by an object.

I **read** the book.

uncountable (noncount) noun A common noun that cannot be counted. A noncount noun has no plural form and cannot occur with *a, an,* or a number.

information mathematics weather

verb A word that refers to an action or a state.

Ahn **closed** the window.
Miguel **loves** classical music.

verb phrase A phrase that has a main verb and any objects, adverbs, or dependent clauses that complete the meaning of the verb in the sentence.

Who **called you**?
He **walked slowly.**

Appendix IV | Correlation to *Grammar Sense 1*

EFFECTIVE ACADEMIC WRITING 1: THE PARAGRAPH	*GRAMMAR SENSE 1*
UNIT 2 Adjectives *Be* to Define and Describe	**CHAPTER 6** Descriptive Adjectives **CHAPTER 1** Simple Present Statements with *Be*
UNIT 3 The Simple Present	**CHAPTER 9** The Simple Present
UNIT 4 Imperatives Modals of Advice, Necessity, and Prohibition	**CHAPTER 3** Imperatives **CHAPTER 22** Modals of Advice, Necessity, and Prohibition
UNIT 5 The Simple Past The Past Continuous	**CHAPTER 12** The Simple Past **CHAPTER 13** The Past Continuous
UNIT 6 *There is/There are* to Introduce Facts	**CHAPTER 16** *There Is* and *There Are*